Paying the Piper: Subsidies, Politics, and the Environment

DAVID MALIN ROODMAN

April Bowling, *Research Intern*

Jennifer Mitchell, *Staff Researcher*

Jane A. Peterson, *Editor*

WORLDWATCH PAPER 133
December 1996

FINANCIAL SUPPORT is provided by Carolyn Foundation, the Nathan Cummings Foundation, the Geraldine R. Dodge Foundation, The Ford Foundation, the George Gund Foundation, The William and Flora Hewlett Foundation, W. Alton Jones Foundation, John D. and Catherine T. MacArthur Foundation, Andrew W. Mellon Foundation, The Curtis and Edith Munson Foundation, The Pew Charitable Trusts, Lynn R. and Karl E. Prickett Fund, Rasmussen Foundation, Rockefeller Brothers Fund, Rockefeller Financial Services, Surdna Foundation, Turner Foundation, U.N. Population Fund, Wallace Genetic Foundation, Wallace Global Fund, Weeden Foundation, and the Winslow Foundation.

Table of Contents

The views expressed are those of the author(s) and do not necessarily represent those of the Worldwatch Institute, its directors, officers, or staff, or of its funding organizations.

ACKNOWLEDGMENTS: I thank Douglas Koplow, André de Moor, Norman Myers, Ronald Steenblik, and the entire Worldwatch research staff for comments on earlier drafts of this paper that helped raise the quality of the final draft several notches. I am grateful also to scores of people who have shared knowledge culled from vast experience with the many issues and regions affected by subsidies. And thanks to Lori Ann Baldwin and Laura Malinowski for responding quickly to many requests for books and articles; to Jennifer Seher for turning typescript into polished page proofs; and to Jim Perry, Denise Byers Thomma, and Tara Patterson for media outreach. April Bowling and Jennifer Mitchell performed research with unfailing good humor, energy, and precision. And Jane Peterson's thoughtful comments made editing a pleasure and an education.

Lastly, I thank Hoangmai Pham, my wife, who has given the most for the sake of this paper, measured in lost time together during a difficult summer. As I finished the project, we each mourned the passing of a mentor: two people who inspired us by touching the lives of so many others as well as our own. This paper is dedicated to the memories of teacher Arthur Benjamin and minister Francis Kensill.

DAVID MALIN ROODMAN is a Research Associate at the Worldwatch Institute, where he investigates the economics and political economy of environmental problems. He has written about energy policy, the human and ecological impacts of buildings, and the use of taxes and other market mechanisms to protect the environment. He contributes regularly to the Institute's annuals, *State of the World* and *Vital Signs*, and to its magazine, *World Watch*. Mr. Roodman graduated from Harvard College with a Bachelor's in pure mathematics. He then spent a year at the University of Cambridge, U.K., where his interests shifted to the relationships between economies and the environment.

Introduction

The "polluter pays principle" is an idea with which it is hard to quibble. Simply put, when we act in ways that hurt the environment—when we harm other people, property, or nature itself through pollution or resource depletion—we ought to be held accountable for the damage we do. This is a matter not just of fairness, but of sound economics. For when we do not pay, we are insulated from the environmental costs pollution imposes on others, and tend to behave as if those costs did not exist. This encourages people to contaminate the air, soil, and water with little concern for neighbors, and to consume resources with little thought for the future. And when the natural environment suffers, the human economy that depends on it suffers too.

Yet as much sense as it makes, "polluter pays" is less the order of the day in most societies than "paying the polluter." Around the world, governments offer myriad subsidies for activities that end up harming the environment and wasting money, thus weakening economies.

In post-communist Russia, home energy prices are kept at an eightieth or less of world levels in an inefficient attempt to hold down the cost of living. The rich, who use the most heat, are saving the most money. And because of a long tradition of cheap energy, residential buildings generally lack thermostats, which forces tenants to cool overheated apartments in winter by opening windows. This contributes to a host of environmental problems, from the overly rapid depletion of Russia's vast natural gas reserves to high greenhouse gas emission rates.[1]

In California's Central Valley, some farmers can buy a thousand cubic meters of water from a federal project—enough to irrigate a few hundred square meters of vegetables—for $2.84, even though it costs the government $24.84 to deliver it. Thanks to fertile soil and favorable climate, however, the water is actually worth at least $80–160 in the valley, based on what farmers pay for water from the state government. Although it was originally meant to give small farms in the United States a financial boost (perhaps not one as big as this), cheap water also benefits many large farms. Idaho billionaire J.R. Simplot continues to build his fortune using subsidized water from the Columbia River to turn arid lands into vast potato farms supplying the likes of McDonald's. In a region where this precious resource is scarce and salinization and other side effects of improper irrigation are becoming increasingly serious, low prices are encouraging farmers to squander water rather than husband it.[2]

Worldwide, government policies shunt at least $500 billion a year toward activities that harm the environment, from overfishing to driving cars and trucks. The full amount may be far greater: few countries have even tried to assess the magnitude of the subsidies they create, and of those that have, none have fully succeeded. Moreover, the most valuable subsidies, such as free insurance against nuclear accidents and the transfer of grazing rights from traditional owners to commercial interests, are often the most difficult to measure. With the global tax burden standing at roughly $7.5 trillion a year, subsidies effectively elevate taxes—on wages, profits, and consumer spending—by at least 7 percent and perhaps much more. Increased taxes on work, investment, and consumption in turn discourage these activities, placing drag on the global economy. And this in an era of supposed worldwide fiscal austerity.[3]

As one would expect, some of the financial costs of subsidies reach the public through higher taxes. In some cases, however, the costs' transmission path bypasses the government treasury altogether. For example, by manipulating food prices—by raising them—governments in western industrial countries transfer $122 billion of wealth each year from food buyers to food sellers, including many millionaire farmers and a few billion-dollar agricultural companies. For consumers, this hidden "cross-subsidy" is just a tax by another name.[4]

An enumeration of the side effects of all these subsidies virtually catalogs today's environmental problems. Subsidies for logging and mining accelerate forest degradation and water pollution. Those for coal production directly add to local problems such as land disturbance and water pollution while contributing on a global scale to atmospheric concentrations of heat-trapping carbon dioxide. Agricultural subsidies in industrial countries have been found to correlate with higher rates of pesticide and fertilizer use, thus increasing water pollution and soil degradation. The list of adverse effects of subsidies continues on, from smog to nuclear waste generation. (See Table 1.)

Governments, of course, rarely set out to degrade the environment when they create these subsidies. Rather, they offer most of them in the name of such causes as stimulating economic development, protecting communities dependent on resource-intensive industries, enhancing national security by reducing dependence on imports of commodities such as oil, and helping the poor.

Thus it is conceivable that many of these subsidies could be justifiable, despite their environmental and financial costs. Unfortunately, however, it is hard to find a subsidy for environmentally destructive activities that does much good at reasonable cost. Some strive for obsolete or questionable goals. Mining and grazing subsidies that some governments long ago instituted to encourage European settlement of territories taken from indigenous peoples are one example. Other subsidies are largely ineffective—for instance, nuclear power technology is foundering despite the tens of billions of dollars that taxpayers have poured into it. Still others have been undone by the very environmental destruction they encouraged. Subsidies designed to

TABLE 1
Selected Subsidies That Have Harmful Side Effects, By Activity

Activity	Examples of Subsidies	Side Effects
Mineral production	Low or zero royalties on oil and other minerals; aid for coal production in Germany, Russia, and other industrial countries	Stimulatory effects of low royalties are minimal; but those of subsidies to uncompetitive industries are significant, abetting pollution and waste
Logging	Low timber royalties in developing countries; below-cost sales in North America and Australia	Stimulatory effects of low royalties are minimal; but below-cost sales worsen deforestation, siltation, and floods
Fishing	Billions of dollars per year in subsidies for fuel, equipment, and income support for fishers worldwide	Promote overfishing, thus hurting catch, employment, and marine ecosystems in the long run
Agricultural inputs	$13 billion a year lost on public irrigation projects in developing countries; billions more lost in industrial ones; subsidies for pesticides and fertilizers in some developing countries	Encourage water waste and salinization, higher rates of pesticide and fertilizer use, soil degradation, and water pollution
Crop and livestock production	$302 billion in annual support for farmers in western industrial countries; low fees for grazing on public lands in North America and Australia; tax breaks for forest clearance in Brazil until 1988	Encourage environmentally destructive farming and overgrazing
Energy use	$101 billion in fossil fuel and power subsidies in developing countries each year; comparable losses in rest of world	Contribute to energy-related problems ranging from particulate emissions to global warming

| Driving | Excess of $111 billion a year in U.S. in costs of roads, related services, and tax breaks over what drivers pay in fuel taxes and other fees | Encourage low-density, car-based land use patterns, contributing to oil import dependence, smog, and traffic jams |

Source: Worldwatch Institute, based on sources cited in text.

support the fishing industry, for example, have only accelerated overfishing and fishery collapse. Most others, like those for heating fuel in Russia, reach their intended beneficiaries to some extent, but only inefficiently. Much of the money leaks into the hands of people who need it less.

In sum, these subsidies as currently implemented invite a four-pronged indictment: they increase the cost of government; the higher taxes they engender discourage work and investment; they fail on their own terms; and they hurt the environment.

The case for reform is thus compelling. What shape reform should take, however, is a much more complex issue. The subsidies with goals no longer deemed worthwhile or achievable ought to be phased out. But there is a stronger case for retaining, in some form and for some time, a number of those meant to enhance national security, to stabilize communities dependent on resource-based industries, or to aid the poor. Even here though, because the subsidies are now so crudely targeted, there is ample room for cutbacks and restructuring that can help the environment, save money, and improve subsidy effectiveness. Finally, carefully designed support for environmentally *constructive* activities, such as the commercialization of energy-efficient technologies, also deserves emphasis in reformed subsidy policies—though other policies, such as regulations and pollution taxes, must ultimately play the larger role here.

Overall, thoroughgoing reform would further the intended goals of current subsidies, eliminate most of their financial costs, and help protect the environment. As subsidies fell so too would taxes. Some goods, such as food in western industrial countries, would become cheaper. Urban air would be safer to breathe and rural groundwater safer to drink. More developing countries would mimic the successes of South Korea and Taiwan, whose economies have grown thanks more to investment in education than subsidization of resource extraction. In industrial countries, environmental *protection*, more than *exploitation*, would become the watchword of economic development: regions once dependent on increasingly automated industries like logging and mining would attract the sorts of job-intensive service businesses that can locate anywhere—and will go wherever the quality of life is highest.

The greatest challenge for reformers may not be figuring out what reform should look like, but making it a political reality. The direct beneficiaries of environmentally harmful subsidies, such as middle-class buyers of cheap electricity or investors and workers in resource-based industries, often have more legal recognition, are better organized and financed, or are collectively more self-aware than those harmed, who may include low-income or indigenous people, city dwellers who cannot tell what is in the air they breathe or where it comes from, generations yet unborn—and, of course, general taxpayers. As a result, subsidy recipients are more adept at exploiting avenues of political influence such as public protests, campaign contributions, family connections, and even corruption in order to thwart change. Subsidy reform, then, and more generally, continuing progress toward environmental sustainability, are bound up with the broader task of making government more equally accountable to all the governed.

Many countries have already engaged in some subsidy reduction, restructuring, and retargeting in order to reduce costs and environmental damage, despite resistance from vested interests. Fiscal crises in the former Eastern bloc and in many debt-hobbled developing countries, for example, have made some of the largest subsidies, such as those for energy and fertilizer, unaffordable in the 1990s, leading to major across-the-board cuts. A dozen or more developing countries also offer "lifeline rates"—discounts on the first, modest increment of electricity bought each month—that target some electricity subsidies at the poor rather than all recipients, as is more usual. Among developed countries, Belgium, France, and Japan have slowly phased out most or all of their subsidies for domestic coal production (though they have maintained many other subsidies). Grants, foreign aid, and tax breaks have helped create thriving wind-power industries in Denmark and India and solar panel markets in the Dominican Republic.[5]

But the political resilience of subsidies should not be underestimated. Especially in western industrial countries, many subsidies that reward environmental destruction remain in place despite rising public debt and growing concern about the environment. And as those countries now in fiscal crisis restore budgetary stability, pressures for reform at the global level could easily flag. Yet finishing the job of subsidy reform is an essential first step toward ensuring a just future for our children. It makes little sense for societies to begin making the polluter pay until they first stop paying the polluter.

Subsidies: What, How, and Why

Few government policies are as unpopular in theory and as popular in practice as subsidies. The very word can cause economists to shudder, make taxpayers fume, deepen the cynicism of the poor, and enrage environmentalists. Yet to judge by the budgets and natural resource policies of governments around the world, subsidies are in permanent fashion.

An array of techniques for shaping economic activity lie at the disposal of today's policymakers. They can stimulate an economy by cutting taxes and launching jobs programs, or slow it down by hiking short-term interest rates. They can issue rules to regulate industry. They can tax activities they want to discourage, such as buying cigarettes or polluting the air. And finally, they can subsidize certain groups, using some of the vast lands and funds at their disposal.

A subsidy is defined here as a government policy that alters market risks, rewards, and costs in ways that favor certain activities or groups. The most visible subsidies are direct government payments that help hold down prices for consumers or prop them up for producers. Subsidies also take a dizzying variety of less obvious forms that are actually more popular with politicians because of their low visibility and can be just as costly. Many subsidies, for example, accrue through special tax breaks. Whether subsidies elevate government spending or reduce government income, though, it is the general taxpayer—or more precisely, the un-subsidized taxpayer—that must ultimately bear the costs.

Subtle subsidies also arise when governments sell services and resources for less than it costs to provide them (as in the case of most public irrigation water) or for less than they are worth (low interest charges on loans for ranching in the rainforest, for instance). Or to take another nearly universal example, despite the accumulating reams of free trade treaties, most governments still aid domestic industries with tariffs and import quotas. The cost of protection mostly passes on to consumers through higher prices. The U.S. government, for instance, uses trade restrictions to help keep domestic sugar prices at twice the world level, costing consumers $1.4 billion per year. But high sugar prices also provide a powerful stimulus for cane production in the Florida Everglades wetlands, thereby contributing heavily to the pollution and degradation of this ecosystem. (Heaping insult upon injury, the government will spend another $200 million of taxpayers' money between 1996 and 2002 trying to repair the very damage to the Everglades that it has abetted.)[6]

Another important but difficult-to-evaluate subsidy results when governments take on private risks. Early in the history of civilian nuclear power, for example, the U.S. government capped utilities' liability for damage from nuclear power plant accidents and assumed the rest itself, free of charge. Since the likelihood and costs of a nuclear accident are impossible to evaluate reliably, no private insurance company will take on the risk. Without this ongoing subsidy the industry might never have developed and could not operate today. The subsidy is thus, in a sense, invaluable to the industry.[7]

Similarly incalculable are the cross-subsidies that occur when public authorities dedicate government-controlled land to commercial activities such as logging or mining at the expense of alternative uses—say, the life-sustaining activities of indigenous peoples—that may be less commercially competitive but not necessarily less worthwhile. Indeed the very idea of economic value begins to stretch thin when extended to such forced transfers of property rights. For economic value is based on the assumption of *voluntary* exchange: to say that something is worth a thousand dollars is to say that people would freely surrender it for that. How does one, for example, calculate the costs in dollar terms to indigenous Dayak people in the Malaysian state of Sarawak of the loss of forests on their homelands, which the government has brought about by sanctioning large-scale logging by outsiders?[8]

It might seem obvious that all of these subsidies actually encourage the activities they reward. The less risky, the cheaper, or the more profitable an activity is, the more it will occur—or so it would seem. And, indeed, this is usually the case. But sometimes subsidies are not needed to make an economically attractive activity more attractive, or they fail to make an economically unattractive activity any less unattractive. In the United States, for example, free liability insurance did nothing to halt the collapse of the nuclear power plant market in the 1970s.[9]

The desired ends of government support are as various as their means. Historically, subsidies and cross-subsidies for environmentally harmful behavior have been avowedly aimed at achieving widely accepted collective goals. In some countries, for instance, aid for miners, loggers, and ranchers has been justified as speeding regional economic develop- ment. Coal and agriculture subsidies are supposed to stabi- lize rural communities. Incentives for domestic oil produc- tion are meant to promote energy independence. Across- the-board price reductions on fuel and water, nearly ubiqui- tous outside the industrial west, aim to ease the plight of the poor.

Some conservatives attack all subsidies as market manipulations destined to do more harm than good. Giving free play to Adam Smith's "invisible hand," they argue, is the best way to make the economy work for society. But there are good reasons to subsidize. Real economies never perform as perfectly as the unfettered ones in economic the- ories. One of their most widely acknowledged flaws is the tendency toward oligopoly: the dominance of an industry by a few large companies, which tends to reduce competi- tion and innovation over the long run. And even if such flaws could be corrected, economists acknowledge that what they term efficient outcomes in textbooks—those that max- imize material wealth—can end up working against collec- tive visions of how society should be shaped, by allowing abject poverty to continue, for example. Both shortcomings of the market—its imperfections in practice, and its inade- quacies even in theory—give cause for government inter- vention.[10]

Nevertheless, the impulse behind conservatives' skepti- cism is a healthy one. It is important to examine existing and proposed subsidies carefully for effectiveness and worth. To the extent that subsidies serve obsolete ends, reach unin- tended beneficiaries, create unintended incentives, or gener- ate exorbitant costs to achieve reasonable benefits, they impose a double economic burden. First, they incur direct costs in the form of higher prices and higher taxes on wages and earnings, which shortchange the consumer and general taxpayer and also handicap economies by discouraging work, investment, and consumption. Second, the flawed subsidies inflict indirect costs on people's health and property through environmental destruction.

To be most effective, subsidies need to be sharply targeted. They should reach only those meant to be helped. They should cease when they are no longer needed. Most fundamentally, their benefits should justify their full direct and indirect costs. (See Table 2.) Such principles are straightforward. Yet the reality is that few subsidies obey them. Many are ineffective or, because of poor targeting, inefficient, especially once the full direct and indirect costs are considered.

For purposes of closer analysis, subsidies with major environmental effects can be roughly broken into five categories, based on the policy goals best ascribed to them: stimulating overall economic development; protecting domestic industries for the sake of national security or workers; cutting costs for consumers, particularly low-income consumers; funding infrastructure out of general revenues; and

TABLE 2
Six Principles of Good Subsidy Policy

- Subsidies may be warranted if they make markets work more efficiently, for example, by overcoming barriers to the commercialization of new technologies, or by favoring environmentally benign technologies over ones with hidden environmental costs.

- Subsidies may be warranted if they advance societal values other than economic efficiency, such as slowing the disintegration of company towns or feeding the poor.

- Subsidies should be effective.

- Subsidies should be efficient: they should directly and exclusively target intended beneficiaries.

- Subsidies should be the least-cost means of achieving their purpose.

- All costs, including environmental costs, should be counted when weighing the worth of subsidies. This entails sometimes-difficult judgments about how to compare different kinds of harms and benefits.

Source: Worldwatch Institute.

developing new technologies. Almost all of these subsidies are ripe for reform through better targeting toward intended recipients, shifts to new ones, or complete phaseouts. Of course what actually keeps these subsidies in place may have more to do with politics than policy, but taking them at face value provides a starting point for analysis. Then, as a separate matter, their political underpinnings can be examined.

Perpetuating the Cowboy Economy

In 1966, at a time when humanity was still absorbing the shock of seeing its world for the first time in pictures from space, economist Kenneth Boulding predicted that the sudden perception of earth as a finite world spinning in an inhospitable universe would eventually penetrate the very workings of modern societies. The "cowboy" economies that increasingly characterized human civilization, ones that treated natural resources as inexhaustible, were on a collision course with environmental limits. The day would come when they would need to transform into "spaceman" economies that, somewhat as astronauts do, would respect tight environmental limits, conserving resources and recycling waste. The longer societies delayed embarking upon this transition, Boulding noted, the more difficult it would be, and the longer economies would tear at their own environmental supports.[11]

The oldest and perhaps most environmentally destructive subsidies are the ones that effectively deny the inevitability of this transformation: they artificially stimulate resource-intensive industries such as logging, mining, and livestock raising in the name of economic growth. The roots of modern subsidies for such activities lie in the histories of the nations settled by European emigrants, including Australia, Canada, and the United States. With their frontier days over, the special supports these countries once gave such industries are ever harder to justify. Yet many of the subsidies live on, burdening taxpayers and accelerating environmental destruction. Meanwhile developing countries, seeking to replicate the material success of colonies that gained independence long before they did, have also begun transferring large amounts of resources from traditional ownership to more commercial interests.

In North America and Australia, most natural resource policy dates to the second half of the nineteenth century and the early twentieth century, when the space and natural resources in newly acquired territories seemed empty and inexhaustible. From this perspective, the natural solution was to offer the minerals, timber, water, and land as inducements to would-be colonists, usually free. In the United States, these policies also resonated with the Jeffersonian ideal of the yeoman farmer—or small-time miner or rancher—come to conquer the wilderness, improve the land, and build a better life and a great nation. As settlers scattered eagerly across the land, they staked and defended claims to gold deposits, rangeland, and waterways—it was first come, first served. As governments gradually caught up with them, formalizing resource law, they generally ratified existing arrangements, locking into place enormous and ongoing transfers of wealth. Many of these subsidies—although they involve governments giving away or selling resources for less than they cost to provide or less than they are worth (practices that would be folly for any private business)—are so embedded in the cultural landscape that recipients no longer see them for what they are.[12]

Over its history, the U.S. government alone has given away 400 million hectares—half the country's continental expanse—and offers cheap access to millions more for certain resource-based activities. Hardrock mining is still essentially free on a large fraction of public land in the United States and Canada. In 1994, for instance, a Canadian concern bought 790 hectares of federal land in Goldstrike, Nevada, for $5,190; the tract contained gold worth $10 billion once mined—2 million times as much as it paid. All told, since 1873 U.S. taxpayers have forgone roughly $242 billion (in 1995 dollars) in potential mineral royalties on federal lands, equal to $900 per U.S. citizen and enough to pay off a twentieth of the accumulated federal debt, according to the Mineral Policy Center in Washington, D.C. They have also accepted an estimated $33–72 billion in liability for environmental cleanup at abandoned mines.[13]

As impressive as these figures are, the true subsidy here consists of usurping millions of hectares of land from indigenous peoples and zoning it for mining. The failure to charge market rates for minerals on public land is one instance where a subsidy may not actually stimulate what it rewards. After all, even if governments sold off mineral rights at full market value, they would, by definition, only be charging what mining companies were willing to pay for them—and still mine just as much.

A different picture emerges when governments start spending taxpayers' money assisting resource-based industries on public lands. In fact, some governments actually expend large sums assisting livestock and timber operations in the public domain—often more than they earn in grazing fees and timber royalties. Were these costs passed back to the beneficiaries, logging and grazing on much public land would become unprofitable, and would cease. The U.S. and British Columbian governments, for example, lose millions of dollars administering public rangelands, only in part because they lease the lands at roughly a third of private rates. Government timber sales in parts of the United States and Australia, especially where young trees or steep terrain make logging expensive, bring in less than agencies spend managing the concessions, particularly building logging roads.[14]

In the United States, an almost Stalinist planning process drives these losses. Every year, Congress sets a timber production quota for public lands as part of the budgeting process. This target then percolates down through the pyramid-like Forest Service bureaucracy until it reaches the level of local foresters, who must then do whatever it takes to fill their share of the quota, from building roads in once-road-less wilderness to requiring loggers to clear-cut. Annual losses on forest administration hovered in the range of $300–400 million in the United States in the early 1990s, according to Randal O'Toole, an economist and director of the Thoreau Institute in Oak Grove, Oregon, who examines the agency's books. In effect, the general taxpayer is paying timber companies to raze public forests.

The biggest money-loser is the Tongass National Forest in Alaska, the world's largest remaining temperate rain forest. Providing roads and other services to private clear-cutting operations there cost the government $389 million between 1982 and 1988, yet earned it only $32 million. In the Australian state of Victoria, the pattern is strikingly similar: there the government is losing some $170 million a year on net. Losses like these lead to the perverse conclusion that taxpayers would be better off banning such resource-intensive activities on many public lands and splitting the savings with industry—in other words, paying ranchers not to ranch and loggers not to log.[15]

In the United States, an almost Stalinist planning process drives losses on public forests.

There is little doubt that these generous resource giveaways have met their historical purpose of spurring European settlement of the New World. Indeed, they have contributed mightily to a transformation of cultural and physical landscapes. Thousands of indigenous communities have been eliminated or squeezed onto small reservations. The ranges of many native species, such as the buffalo, have also shrunk to fragments. In the continental United States, 95 percent of the forests, including most public ones, have been logged at least once. In Australia and the arid American West, overgrazing of cattle has robbed land of much vegetative cover, freeing soils to erode and turning thousands of streams into muddy gullies.[16]

But since these subsidies were adopted, many of the economies of regions once dominated by resource-intensive

industries have undergone dramatic transformations, making the subsidies increasingly archaic. Small-time miners
and loggers have given way to mining and logging multinationals—established companies that, like other firms, should
largely be expected to stand or fall on their own. In the
resource-rich states of Idaho, Oregon, and Washington and
the province of British Columbia, 1 in 12 workers made a
living quarrying minerals, felling trees, or milling lumber in
1969; in 1993, 1 in 25 did. Meanwhile, a new breed of set-
tler is appearing. Service and manufacturing companies are
moving in, attracted by the quality of the natural environment. In the United States, western counties with open
space are among the fastest growing in the country. Public
attitudes reflect this economic shift. A recent poll in the
United States reported that 59 percent of adults opposed
expanding mining and grazing on public lands; just 26 percent supported it.[17]

Though industrial countries have reached something
of a dead end on the cowboy-style economic path, poorer
countries have eagerly followed in their footsteps. As the
colonial era finally came to a close at mid-century, the new
governments in Latin America, Africa, and developing Asia
adopted patterns of resource ownership and management
from their colonial rulers. They claimed 80 percent of the
world's tropical forests from traditional residents and owners, equally high shares of the minerals and water within
their borders, and much of the land as well. Many began
cashing in these natural resources, usually for much less
than they were worth, hoping to jump-start economic
growth.[18]

One indicator of the eagerness to liquidate natural
wealth has been the rising output from resource-intensive
industries in developing countries. They now mine four
times as much unprocessed copper concentrate as they did
in 1955, pump six times as much oil, and fell seven times as
much timber for non-fuel use. (See Figure 1.)[19]

Surprisingly, although policymakers have usually
argued that transfers of resources into the hands of com-

FIGURE 1

Production of Selected Primary Commodities, Developing Countries, 1955–95

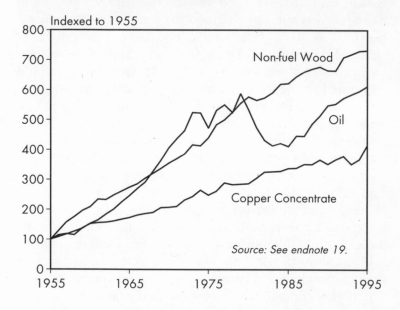

Source: See endnote 19.

mercial industries stimulate economic growth, the results generally have been slower growth and more poverty. The more a developing country's economy depended on primary resource exports in 1971—that is, the more it seemingly played off of its inherited strengths—the less it had grown in per capita terms by 1989, according to a statistical analysis by Jeffrey Sachs and Andrew Warner, economists at Harvard University. On average, in fact, a 17 percentage point increase in the share of primary resource exports in gross domestic product (GDP) in 1971 corresponded to a 1 percentage point fall in average annual growth over the period. Meanwhile resource-poor countries like South Korea and Taiwan experienced robust and lasting economic growth.[20]

In developing nations more than in western industrial countries, the key subsidy for extractive industries has not been the low prices frequently charged for access to government-controlled resources but the often unilateral transfers to commercial interests of resource rights from the ancient indigenous peoples who are the traditional owners. Even if governments had charged market rates for these natural assets, and even if they had used the earnings to compensate previous owners, this would not have fundamentally changed the outcome. The market would still have willingly bought up the resources, and many local people would still have lost the use of their land against their wishes.

Charging low prices for access to public resources has, however, meant much less potential funding for public investment in infrastructure, education, public health, and family planning—the very sort of funding that developing countries routinely seek from the World Bank and international donors. The forgone revenues have often been glaring in the logging industry. Finding and cutting timber—which is not much harder than taking a walk in the woods—can be a quick, profitable business, making cheap logging concessions ideal for political patronage. For example, the government in Indonesia, a country pervaded by corruption, has sold timber concessions at a third or less of market value on a third of the country's territory since the late 1960s. In 1990, it captured only 17 percent of the value of timber sold, earning $416 million. If the ratio of real to potential revenues had matched that for its oil concessions—85 percent—the government would have earned another $2.1 billion, equal to 40 percent of its foreign aid that year. Instead, the money mostly wound up in the bank accounts of a dozen or so timber magnates with close ties to President Suharto and his family. Concession prices have been similarly low among other tropical timber exporters, including Côte d'Ivoire, Ghana, Malaysia, and the Philippines, largely because of close ties between industry and policymakers.[21]

In the case of minerals such as oil, financial losses have also often been significant, if less premeditated. The expensive risks in minerals exploration and the technical complexities of mining and drilling make it much more difficult for cronies of the powerful to jump into such businesses. As a result, experienced and well-financed multinationals based in industrial countries have played a much bigger role in minerals than in timber. And they have often exploited the poor comprehension of these complexities among government negotiators to win inordinately profitable agreements. Over time, however, negotiating skills within a given country have generally improved with experience. This is why Indonesia was able to raise its share of the windfall profits from oil production from 65 percent in the late 1960s, to 85 percent today. It is the countries newest to the international minerals market, such as Guyana, Vietnam, and former Soviet republics, that are now striking the poorest deals.[22]

In Saudi Arabia, economic production per person was higher before the oil boom than after.

As Indonesia has with oil, some countries have captured much of the windfall from natural resource development by charging fair royalties, or nationalizing industries (though state-owned companies are notorious for dissipating windfalls through inefficiency). And some have even spread the earnings equitably among their citizens. But even they have seen slow growth. During the years of expensive oil, for example, exporters such as Venezuela and the Persian Gulf states began using the revenues from highly profitable state oil companies to keep taxes low and fund generous social programs. Yet their economic growth was significantly below average, or even negative. In Saudi Arabia, economic production per person was actually higher before the oil boom than after, despite a windfall of some $500 billion. As inherited wealth often does, this bounty seems generally to have blunted the drive for economic self-improvement rather than fueled it.[23]

The causes of this paradox are the subject of much debate among economists and political scientists. Several important factors appear to contribute. One is that the leaps and dives of commodity prices can afflict resource-depen-

dent countries with economic whiplash: episodes of high
prices lead to ambitious, sometimes hasty investment plans;
later, low prices force governments to choose between
ruinous budget deficits and useless, half-finished projects.
Another is that the governments have often spent much of
their windfalls on politically popular subsidies for things
like gasoline at the expense of the investments in education
and healthcare that would have done more for long-term
economic development.[24]

More fundamentally, modern resource production does
less than other industries to stimulate long-term growth in
local economies. Much of the equipment that these enclave-
like industries use is imported from abroad, and the raw
materials they produce are quickly exported. It will be
decades before a country like Bolivia can compete with
industrial countries in the manufacture of the massive,
high-technology mining equipment used within its own
borders. Likewise, in the days of cheap sea transport, infrastructure and technical know-how, not proximity of rain-
forests, are what give a country like Japan an advantage in
the wood-processing business. Thus when a mine plays out
or a forest is depleted, extractive industries withdraw, leaving few constructive reminders of their presence (unless the
government actually charged substantial royalties and
invested them well).[25]

Indeed, since extractive industries are particularly hard
on the environment, their longest-lasting local effects are
often the destructive ones. In Ecuador and Nigeria, oil production has poisoned the water and farmlands of local peoples, or completely displaced them. Metal mining has filled
rivers in Guyana and Papua New Guinea with silt and heavy
metals, killing fish and permanently contaminating river-
side cropland. Fencing of grazing lands for commercial cattle ranchers in Botswana has cut into the traditional range
of native pastoralists. Perhaps most destructive of all have
been the conflicts over forests, because of the vast areas they
cover and the rich biodiversity they contain. From Brazil to
Côte d'Ivoire to the Solomon Islands, government sanction

of logging and incentives for forest clearance by ranchers and farmers have contributed substantially to deforestation, species loss, and the disintegration of indigenous cultures.[26]

Experiences in the Indonesian province of East Kalimantan illustrate how an extractive industry can actually harm a regional economy. The timber industry there has brought employment to 6 percent of the potential workforce, but it has destroyed even more jobs by depriving cottage industries of forest access, according to the Indonesian Forum for the Environment (WALHI) in Jakarta. In 1989, for instance, the village of Jelmu Sibak found itself encircled by two government-granted timber concessions. Villagers were cut off from much of the land on which they normally cultivated rice, honey, fruit, rattan, and other crops. Under government pressure, the concessionaires gave residents modest cash handouts, a new road, and satellite television. A few villagers also got logging jobs. This did not compensate, however, for the substantial, permanent reduction in the village's source of livelihood. In Jelmu Sibak, as in East Kalimantan as a whole, the standard of living fell during the late 1980s and early 1990s.[27]

As in industrial countries, natural resource subsidies in the developing world have done little to address contemporary economic priorities. Because they have rarely worked, and because they have often worsened the situation of the poorest of the poor, government resource giveaways need to be scaled back. The track record of most such subsidies in terms of slow growth, environmental damage, and impoverishment and violation of the human rights of local peoples is abysmal. Economies and societies would be better off if local peoples were granted more control over their lands, and if resources were always sold at full value in order to fund education, health care, and infrastructure—all vital ingredients in sustainable and equitable economic development.

Dikes Against a Rising Sea

Though most resource extraction subsidies have been defended in the name of economic progress, some have served a more conservative impulse: to stem the economic tide when it turns against a resource-based industry. The two most common rationales for protectionism are that it saves consumers from the apparent dangers of import dependence and shields workers from job loss. Yet however well intended, these subsidies, like most, have usually been unnecessary, poorly implemented, or doomed by circumstances to failure.

In the case of subsidies meant to stave off import dependence, too often the shibboleth of "national security" has substituted for careful thinking about when they are really necessary. The concentration of two-thirds of the world's oil reserves in one volatile region is clearly a long-term threat to the economic stability of petroleum importers. But the sources of most other commodities, such as crops and coal, are more evenly spread about the planet, making the dangers of import dependence less clear-cut. Indeed, diversity of supply is often the key to security in the business world. Mineral multinationals, for example, try to reduce their exposure to the risk of political unrest or nationalization of their operations in any one place by developing mines in many parts of the world.[28]

More broadly, trade can increase economic interdependence among nations, and perhaps reduce the likelihood of war or economic embargoes. In this light, it is ironic that the European Union, which was founded on the notion that trade begets security, dedicates most of its budget to what is probably the world's largest protectionist subsidy regime, the Common Agricultural Policy, at $97 billion a year.[29]

In the argument for protectionism on behalf of workers, the starting point has been that farmers, fishers, loggers, and miners have always led particularly insecure lives. Indeed, in recent decades, their jobs have proved more vulnerable than most to the steady march of automation. Worse, in many regions, the industries have literally run themselves into the ground by exhausting the resources on which they depend. That resource-based industries such as logging and coal mining are overwhelmingly rural—giving rise to small, single-industry towns from the Oregon woods to the Russian Arctic coal region of Vorkuta—intensifies the insecurity of individual workers. Often when the job bases shrivel, so do the towns: many families must choose between unemployment and emigration.

Thus industrial nations have often subsidized extractive activities in the belief that economic security for local communities is sometimes worth paying for. It is an especially resonant notion in the industrial world today, where many people feel insecure about their economic futures even though statisticians tell them that their inflation-adjusted incomes have doubled or more since the 1950s. Since people do not seem twice as happy, perhaps some of that income growth is worth trading off for greater economic stability.[30]

Unfortunately, most of the subsidies granted in the name of national security or job security have been far too costly to taxpayers, consumers, and the environment for the amount of good done. One problem—a partly avoidable one—has been clumsy targeting. For example, Germany, Japan, and other industrial countries subsidize domestic coal production by the ton, not the worker. Thus some of the subsidies end up in the pockets of investors, not laborers. As for subsidies in the name of national security, some have actually succeeded only too well, turning the dream of self-sufficiency into a nightmare of costly surpluses.[31]

Government targeting of agriculture subsidies has been perhaps the most ham-handed. A universally echoed rationale for food production subsidies is that they are essential to the preservation of the family farm. Yet such subsidies rarely favor small farmers over large ones and farming corporations. In the United States, for example, despite the intentions of the Depression-era program to shore up the family farm, most payments are based on how much food farmers grow, not on how small their farms are. Not surprisingly, the number of U.S. farms fell by two-thirds between 1930 and 1990, even as grain elevators bulged with millions of tons of surplus food. As a result of this concentration in ownership, 58 percent of the agricultural support payments—$6.5 billion—went to the top 15 percent of farms in 1991, those grossing over $100,000 per year. Farmers in the next 15 percentiles, grossing between $50,000 and $100,000, got another 26 percent of the pie, worth $2.9 billion. This left 17 percent of the money, or $1.9 billion, for the smaller farms (figures in 1995 dollars).[32]

It is true that production subsidies have enhanced the food self-sufficiency of most industrial countries, something particularly valued in the European Union, where memories still linger of wartime scarcities and international supply lines cut off by German U-boats. But the food subsidies have done much more than that. Indeed by the late 1980s, they had turned wartime shortages into mountain-sized surpluses of butter, sugar, and grain. Today chicken, sheep, pigs, and cattle eat 57 percent of the region's grain output. Another 7 percent is exported. Thus people in the European Union are producing three times as much grain as they eat. Clearly the subsidies have gone far beyond ensuring basic food security for the region in times of emergency.[33]

Historically, in all western industrial countries, governments have attempted to limit food surpluses and found themselves drawn into a quicksand of market controls. They began by buying up the surpluses, and taking large losses in dumping them on international markets or even destroying them outright. Dumping depressed global prices, raising the cost of domestic price guarantees even further. To limit costs, countries began requiring farmers to take land out of production, sometimes paying them *not* to farm. Constricting food supply lifted prices, which cost consumers. By 1995, governments in western industrial countries were spending $180 billion of taxpayers' money on agriculture every year, and effectively transferring another

$122 billion from consumers to producers through high prices, for an average total of $22,000 per farmer—with richer farmers getting more. Put otherwise, government policy inflated the annual food budget of a family of four in these countries by an average of $1,500.[34]

Another underappreciated consequence of the rising complexity of food policy has been the concomitant growth in the burden of paperwork and regulations on individual farmers. The profession with one of the most self-reliant images has become one of the most centrally planned sectors of western industrial economies. And some of that planning has played out absurdly at ground level. Brian Chamberlin, former head of the New Zealand Federated Farmers association, described a farm he visited in Scotland in 1992, where subsidies had shifted husbandry from good land to bad:

> The farm had originally been a beautifully balanced livestock unit, with easy rolling land in the front and higher [but poorer-quality] moorland at the back of the property. Grain subsidies came along and the better land was turned over to grain farming, while the livestock was consigned to the poorer land at the back... [W]hen the set-aside arrived, with payments of [$270 per hectare] for doing absolutely nothing with the land, this area was taken out of production... At the same time, hay and grain had to be brought in to feed the hungry (but heavily subsidized) stock on the hill section of the farm.[35]

For all the perversity of such situations, a more serious problem has been that much of the excessive production in industrial countries has come at the expense not only of consumers and taxpayers, but of future production and less fortunate farmers in the rest of the world. Overproduction has depressed food prices in developing countries, which has been good for poor city dwellers there, but disastrous for many unsubsidized farmers. In western industrial nations and formerly communist countries alike, production subsidies have also encouraged environmentally destructive farming, including the use of chemical fertilizers and pesticides and the abandonment of traditional practices such as rotating crops and fallowing fields. These shifts have accelerated soil erosion and the accumulation of chemicals in land and water, threatening the sustainability of agriculture even as global population continues to expand.[36]

The steady erosion of the industry's underlying resource base is a long-term problem in agriculture, but it has reached the crisis stage in fisheries. The global fishing industry appears to have hemorrhaged red ink during most of the 1970s and 1980s, with losses reaching roughly $54 billion in 1989, or 44 percent of expenditures. Much of that gap, though no one knows exactly how much, was probably covered by government subsidies for purchases of boat fuel and fishing equipment, as well as general income support. The collapse of communism in the former Eastern bloc has lowered the global total since then. Yet subsidies are one reason there are now enough boats, hooks, and nets to catch roughly twice the available fish supply, a gross imbalance that continues to generate powerful pressures for overfishing. Thirteen of the 15 major oceanic fisheries are in decline because fish are being hauled in faster than they reproduce. As a result, global oceanic catch today stands at 84 million tons a year, compared with the estimated 100 million that would be available under wiser management. In the increasingly vociferous battles over fishing rights, the livelihoods of the world's 14–20 million small fishers stand in the greatest peril.[37]

Incentives that fail workers and overstimulate output can be amended. But even if they are, many subsidies for resource-based industries will still face daunting odds, for some of the forces that threaten employment and production in domestic industries grow inexorably over the years. Like dikes built against a rising sea, countervailing subsidies have to rise just to stay even. One of these rising pressures threatens employment, not output. Resource-intensive industries are inherently risky, because of dependence on the weather, commodity price swings, and the uncertainties of minerals exploration. Riskiness favors large companies, which can survive lean years more easily than small ones.[38]

The second strike against such industries and their employees is automation, which makes it ever cheaper to substitute capital for labor, and which exploits economies of scale. For example, not only does a modern combine harvester let one pair of hands do the work of many—it also works most economically on large fields. Technologies like these are behind the rapid fall in the number of U.S. farms between 1930 and 1990. And they are not unique to agriculture. The average number of workers needed to fell and mill 9,400 cubic meters of lumber in a year in the United States declined from 20 to 16 during the 1980s. And with the newest mills, the number is only 9. This is a major reason that the U.S. timber industry lost 10,000 jobs during the same period even though the federal government sold enough timber from public forests—much of it below cost— to boost the national harvest to record levels.[39]

What is more, rapid automation in the economy as a whole also threatens resource-intensive industries. This is because the more efficiently a company uses its workers— the more it earns per hour of labor—the higher pay those workers can demand. As a result, companies that boost productivity the slowest will eventually find themselves outbid for workers by those that boost it the fastest. Resource-intensive industries that *fail* to automate quickly can find their wage costs rising faster than earnings, which will eventually drive them out of business.

In industries based on nonrenewable resources, there is a third inexorable trend: the depletion of the resource itself. Multibillion-dollar tax breaks for domestic U.S. oil producers, for example, did not keep their market share from slipping below 50 percent in the 1990s as reserves gradually dwindled. All that such incentives do is shift production from the future, when oil will be scarce, to the present, when it is not.[40]

The hard coal industry in Germany is experiencing
some of these forces in confluence. The country's sole
deposit of hard coal snakes from the Ruhr River to the Dutch
border. As miners have delved ever deeper into this seam,
the costs in time and equipment needed to raise a ton of
coal have climbed, pushing up the price of industry protection. In addition, productivity—output per worker—has
lagged behind the national average, which is one reason
that wages in the industry have climbed much faster than
earnings. In 1982, the government granted the industry $30
in subsidies for each ton of coal it sold in order to bring its
prices within striking distance of imports; by 1995, the figure had nearly quadrupled to $119. Since total subsidies
climbed only a little over half as much—from $2.9 billion to
$6.9 billion—production had to fall 39 percent, and employ-
ment 49 percent. Overall, the cost of protecting a mining
job for a year with per-ton subsidies rose from $15,400 to
$72,800. (See Figure 2.) It would be cheaper now to shut
down the mines and pay miners a handsome salary not to
work. (All figures in 1995 dollars.)[41]

For similar reasons, coal production has been completely phased out in Belgium and nearly so in France,
Japan, and the United Kingdom (though the Japanese industry still received $993 million from the government in
1995). The probability of long-term decline also stalks the
Russian coal industry, which received $3.7 billion in aid in
1994. (All figures in 1995 dollars.)[42]

The costs to society of these subsidized industries
include more than just direct financial outlays. They also
include the indirect environmental costs. For example, agricultural runoff and seepage of fertilizers and pesticides are
major sources of groundwater pollution in many countries.
Studies in the United States and Western Europe have found
clear associations between the level of subsidies in a region
and the amount of farm chemicals used. As societies con-
front such environmental problems, subsidies for the industries that cause them will become increasingly hard to justi-

FIGURE 2

Western German Hard Coal Subsidies and Employment, 1982–95

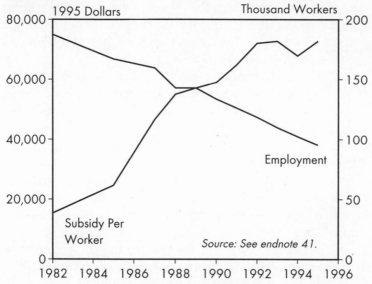

Source: See endnote 41.

fy. In Germany, a country that has made high-profile commitments to reduce its emissions of greenhouse gases and that also needs to cut its federal budget deficit, coal subsidies seem finally to have bumped up against a sort of political limit. Politicians now speak openly of cutting them, or at least halting further rises, portending an acceleration in layoffs in years to come.[43]

The task for policymakers in reforming protectionist subsidies is threefold. First, they need to decide whether protection is needed and can deliver on its promises. In the case of oil production in oil-importing countries, it cannot. Security arguments also generally seem weak for the current levels of support that many countries give to the production of coal, food, and other commodities. Many countries find themselves with surpluses of subsidized commodities, a multiplicity of potential suppliers scattered around the world, or both.

Second, policymakers need to assess the potential gains

from better targeting. In agriculture, just dropping the top-grossing farms from the subsidy rolls would cut budgetary costs dramatically, boost small farms, and reduce the artificial incentive for environmentally destructive farming. Basing the remaining subsidies on income rather than output—in effect converting them to welfare payments—would improve effectiveness even more.

And finally, policymakers need to decide whether, given such improvements, subsidies' benefits are worth the costs. Yet if the financial and environmental costs of subsidies rise steadily over time, it is no longer a question of whether the cost-benefit scale tilts against subsidies, but simply when. Subsidies then have to be seen as tools that cannot hold back the tides of economic change permanently, but only slow their advance in order to give people more time to adapt. They need, in other words, to be seen as transitional.

There are no formulas for performing these cost-benefit comparisons or determining exactly how fast transitional subsidies should be ended. Clearly though, it is generally best if subsidy phaseouts that seriously threaten single-industry communities or regions occur gradually. In some cases the industries themselves can be shut down quickly while the subsidies continue for a few years, paying for worker retraining and incentives for new business start-ups. Losing a job is hard on a family, and losing an employer in a small community is even worse; but the sooner societies make these course corrections, the more gently they can do it.

Shotgun Subsidies

In 1992, around the time world leaders were signing the first international treaty on global warming at the Earth Summit in Rio de Janeiro, two economists at the World Bank in Washington, D.C., decided to perform a simple mathematical exercise. Bjorn Larsen and Anwar Shah gathered information on what people paid for energy in countries such as the United States, China, and the Soviet Union—those that burned most of the world's fossil fuels, the major source of the greenhouse gas carbon dioxide. They found that particularly in centrally planned countries, coal, oil, and natural gas cost much less than they did on world markets—a sure sign of subsidies. When they multiplied the price differences by the amount of fuel bought, they came up with a staggering figure. Collectively, the signatories to the climate treaty paid their own citizens more than $200 billion in 1991 alone to use fossil fuels and thus to emit carbon dioxide. Only 15 *nations* earned that much in 1991.[44]

Though communist countries were the primary subsidizers of fossil fuels in the early 1990s, almost all countries actually subsidize the resource flows essential to life—energy and water—in the name of holding down the cost of living for consumers. To the extent that these subsidies are intended to help all consumers, they are inevitably inefficient, since many of the same people will have to pay the taxes that fund the subsidies. To the extent that these interventions are meant to help the poor in particular, they stand on somewhat firmer ground. The poor typically spend proportionally more of their income than the rich on basic necessities like fuel, drinking water, and irrigation-fed crops, and so can benefit proportionally more from subsidies for these commodities. In Indonesian cities, for example, the poorest fifth of households spend 15 percent of their income on energy for lighting and cooking, while the top fifth spend only 8 percent.[45]

Yet like subsidies meant to protect resource-based employment, most subsidies intended to help the poor suffer from clumsy targeting. They are, in effect, shotgun subsidies, brought about through across-the-board price controls that benefit the rich at least as much as the poor. Since there are other, more effective and efficient ways to aid the poor, ways that do not hurt the environment, these subsidies seem greatly overused. They may deserve a role in national budgets, but not one nearly so large.

As Larsen and Shah reported, governments in the former Eastern bloc spent lavishly to hold down the apparent price of energy. According to figures updated in 1995, these countries spent $135–180 billion in 1991—some 10 percent of their GDP—to keep fuel costs to just a fraction of what they were in the West. Electricity subsidies totaled another $34–39 billion. Not surprisingly, signs of energy waste abounded, from grossly inefficient factories to overheated apartment buildings where residents' only way of cooling off in winter was to open windows. Since then, however, market reforms and tight budgets have led these countries to phase out many subsidies. In Russia, energy prices for industry approached world levels in 1995, which partly explains why energy use and air pollution have dropped sharply. Because industry in formerly communist countries received such a large share of the energy subsidies measured by Larsen and Shah, it also seems likely that the global total has fallen substantially since 1991. But, backed by continuing subsidies, electricity prices for Russian consumers have held steady at 15 percent of world levels, while those for natural gas have actually fallen, from 11 percent of the world rate to an essentially nominal 1 percent.[46]

Developing countries also subsidize energy. They spent an estimated $65 billion in 1991 to fund price controls for fossil fuels, including kerosene, a major heating and lighting source for many low-income people, and diesel fuel, used in the public buses that are an important transport mode for the poor. Controls also drove electricity prices down in developing countries from an average 7.6 cents per kilowatt-hour, where they had stood in the early 1980s, to 5.2 cents by 1988 (in 1995 dollars)—about three-fifths the cost of additional supplies. Developing countries had to grant power companies some $46 billion in handouts in 1991 to cover the losses from low prices, but this did not always stanch the red ink. Moreover, the combination of supply being limited by underfunded utility budgets and demand being stoked by low prices has often led to shortages. In Brazil, the uncertain business climate created by sporadic blackouts cost the economy an estimated $1.7 billion in 1980—three times total revenues in the electricity sector.[47]

Western industrial countries also offer their energy industries financial support. In Italy, government appropriations and tax breaks effectively provide a fifth of the power industry's revenue. In addition to free nuclear accident insurance, the U.S. government offers utilities and fossil fuel producers a clutch of tax breaks worth some $5 billion annually. And it sells power from its own dams and nuclear plants so cheaply that it takes a loss of $4.4 billion each year.[48]

Globally, subsidies for water have also been huge. Indeed, it is almost unheard of for a public water project to come close to covering its costs. In the Murray-Darling river basin, Australia's major agricultural region, most water charges are nominal. The U.S. government spent an estimated $45–93 billion more than it earned on public irrigation projects between 1902 and 1986 (in 1995 dollars). Costs in the former Soviet Union were similarly massive. In developing countries such as China, India, and Pakistan, public water projects lose an estimated $13 billion annually.[49]

It is almost unheard of for a public water project to come close to covering its costs.

Budgetary losses, however, understate the magnitude of many of these subsidies, since water and electricity from many projects are worth more than it costs to deliver them. It might seem fair for governments to charge just enough to cover their costs, and not make a profit even when they could. But selling something for less than it is worth encourages waste and bestows windfalls on resource recipients. Meanwhile, it forces governments to keep conventional taxes higher than they otherwise would need to be, which *does* hurt an economy by discouraging work and investment. That farmers like the ones in California's Central Valley are already profiting from water they buy from other sources at prices much higher than the national government's shows that selling water for what it is worth will affect food production much less than one might expect. Thus, these irrigation subsidies emerge as little more than billion-dollar transfers from the pockets of taxpayers to those of a few lucky farmers.[50]

Likewise, if utilities sell power from well-situated dams at cost, not market value—something private, unregulated companies would never do—they lead consumers to believe that additional supplies will be just as cheap, and consumers respond accordingly. For example, in the United States, electricity prices were estimated to be 27 percent below market value on average in 1984, resulting in projected forgone income of $89 billion (1995 dollars) and boosting electricity use an estimated 37 percent over what it would have been had utilities operated like most private businesses.[51]

Low water and power charges have encouraged practices such as electric home heating and the cultivation of water-intensive crops like rice and alfalfa in arid regions— practices that often do not make economic sense once the full value of these resources is accounted for. Excessive power demand has contributed to the many side effects of energy use, from acid rain to global warming. Russian economists, for example, project that complete subsidy removal by 2010 would cut their carbon dioxide emissions by 38 percent, nitrogen oxides by 43 percent, sulfur dioxide by 66 percent, and particulates by 76 percent, compared with what they would be if the old subsidies had remained in place. Likewise, the illusion of cheap water has driven demand for ever more irrigation projects. Yet diverting large fractions of rivers has disrupted aquatic ecosystems by changing the amount and timing of water flows. Meanwhile, flushing large amounts of water through agricultural lands has caused widespread waterlogging and salinization. The long-term repercussions of this practice will be particularly severe in Asia, where population growth is rapid and farmers are already hitting or exceeding the limits of regional water supplies.[52]

Energy subsidies in particular also permeate into other economic sectors, with additional environmental effects, because industries that use energy intensively also tend to be hard on the environment in other ways. For example, energy subsidies make automation, petrochemical fertilizers, and long-distance transportation seem cheaper, thus giving an added boost to large-scale, industrial-style agriculture. They also improve the economics of fishing, mining, chemical production, virgin paper manufacture, and virgin minerals processing. In the northwestern United States, some $146–389 million per year of the government's various energy subsidies have benefited a handful of large aluminum smelters, members of one of the most energy-intensive industries. In recent years, subsidy receipts may actually have exceeded profits. Worldwide, aluminum smelters tend to congregate around sources of subsidized power, putting aluminum recycling at a disadvantage.[53]

Moreover, direct price controls on energy and water help the poor, if that is their intent, only inefficiently. Though higher-income people may spend less on energy, water, and food from irrigated lands relative to their means, they almost always spend more in absolute terms—and so receive more of the subsidies. In Argentina, Chile, Costa Rica, and Uruguay, for example, the richest fifth of the population receives 30–50 percent more in water subsidies than the poorest fifth. The distribution of electricity subsidies tends to be even more skewed toward middle- and upper-income brackets, since these groups have better access to electricity and more appliances.[54]

Even among the poor, the benefits of cheap energy and water often accrue unevenly. Two billion people in developing countries have no electricity; a billion still lack access to clean water at any price. Moreover, particularly in rural areas, many people depend on traditional fuels such as wood and dung, thus missing out on any kerosene subsidies that are meant for them. Similarly, limited access to clean water can result in tremendous disparities in welfare. It is the main reason that waterborne diseases still generate 10 percent of the disease burden in developing countries. One World Bank survey of 16 cities found that residents forced to buy bottled water from street vendors paid 25 times as much on average as those with access to piped supplies. In rural areas, women and children in families without utility connections spend hours each day collecting fuel and water.[55]

Power and water subsidies also tend to accrue inequitably in agriculture. For instance, most public water projects in developing countries have delivered benefits to fertile plains and valleys, which already have the best growing conditions and the most prosperous farmers. Electricity subsidies, which make groundwater pumping cheap, typically create inequities on a more local scale. Within a single village, rich farmers with large plots of land are best positioned to reap the benefits of government intervention because they have the easiest access to credit for investing in electric pumps and wells, and can spread the costs over the largest harvests. In the village of Bhadresar in Gujarat, India, for example, upper castes owned fully 120 of 128 electric pumpsets in 1988, and thus got the lion's share of power subsidies—and the rapidly dwindling water reserve beneath their feet. In drought years, poor farmers without pumps have often been reduced to buying water from their fortunate neighbors, and at high prices, to quench the thirst of both their crops and their families.[56]

Thus, rather than going to consumers in the form of lower food prices, subsidies for irrigation often end up in the hands of wealthier farmers. And to the extent that farmers do pass some of the subsidies on to consumers through lower food prices, only some of the savings reach low-income food buyers. The lesson is a familiar one: unless societies see irrigation, rather than feeding the poor, as an end in itself, subsidizing it is a waste.

Thus, almost all across-the-board supports for energy and water purchases seem badly misdirected. In countries where many still lack access to power and clean water, governments would do better to provide it to the people still without access to these services rather than to cut prices for those who already have it. Where access is nearly universal, and subsidies for energy and water seem a particularly effective way to help low-income people, they should perhaps be retained, but better targeted. Likewise, if societies want to help the poor buy food, then they should subsidize that goal directly and specifically. For without effective targeting, subsidies meant to redistribute wealth toward the poor defeat their own purpose.

Subsidizing Sprawl

S ubsidies for infrastructure can also make their presence felt by shaping where people live and how they move about. Today's buildings would be useless without the pipes, cables, and roads that splay out to them to provide water, gas, electricity, and mobility. Yet when governments bury the costs of these connectors, which vary with length, they encourage sprawl. At issue is not so much whether governments should fund such infrastructure, but which taxpayers they should send the bill to. Unless the people who decide to live far from city or town centers are asked to pay the higher costs of the infrastructure they need, suburban sprawl will appear artificially cheap. Like other factors that encourage car-dependent development, such as low-density zoning laws, making infrastructure appear cheap to its users contributes to pollution, oil dependence, and traffic jams that chew up billions of hours of people's time.

The difference between what road users pay to drive and what roads actually cost varies considerably from nation to nation, because the levels of fuel taxes, vehicle registration and purchase fees, and road tolls also vary. In much of the European Union, gasoline and vehicle taxes and other levies on drivers are high enough to pay for road construction and maintenance. In France, these revenues together actually exceeded road expenditures by $9 billion in 1994. In the mid-1980s, China's road system raised $1.19 for every $1.00 spent, and Turkey's earned $2.17. However, in Argentina, Bangladesh, Bolivia, Mexico, and Tanzania, road user fees covered only 20–50 percent of direct road costs. The ratio was 91 percent in the United States in 1994, leaving $8 billion to be paid from other taxes. In Japan, the deficit was $15 billion.[57]

The automobile is so enmeshed into the fabric of many societies, though, that direct road expenditure figures only scratch the surface of the support governments give driving. The United States, for example, allows companies to give up to $155-a-month's worth of free parking to each employee tax free (compared with only $65 for mass transit coupons), an exemption worth $20 billion a year (1995 dollars). Even more expensive are essential road-related services, such as traffic management, highway patrols, and emergency response teams. Economists at the World Resources Institute (WRI) in Washington, D.C., have extrapolated from calculations for the city of Pasadena, California, to conclude that governments in the United States spend roughly $83 billion a year (1995 dollars) on these services—nearly as much as on the roads themselves. Since governments mostly cover this out of general revenues, residents pay the same regardless of how far they live from schools, shops, offices, bus routes, and train stations—in other words, regardless of how much they drive. In the United States, passing all these costs back to car and truck drivers through fuel taxes would push up the price of a liter of gasoline or diesel by 20 cents (and of a gallon by 78 cents).[58]

All of these hidden cross-subsidies exacerbate the many side effects of heavy automobile dependence. In the United States, gasoline consumption, and thus oil import dependence, have recently reached all-time highs. One study put the total costs of congestion there, counting the value of people's time, fuel wasted by idling engines, and additional traffic accidents, at $100 billion per year. In developing countries, some exploding metropolises are practically strangling in knotted traffic. Perpetual traffic clots in Bangkok have contributed to severe air pollution and have turned the daily commute for many into a three-hour saga, costing some $2.3 billion per year in lost time. The ongoing crisis appears to be scaring off foreign investment and tourism, and has prompted the government to consider a ban on new car registrations until 2001.[59]

If countries like the United States and Thailand are to repair such transportation problems, and if others, particularly developing countries, are to avoid them in the first place, they could start by bringing drivers face to face with the full budgetary costs of roads and related services. This would discourage people from driving unless they felt that the benefit to them was worth the costs of the infrastructure, thus leading to better use of roads overall. When driving costs rise, people not only drive shorter distances but, more importantly, find other ways of getting around, such as taking the train, bicycling, or walking. A pair of rail lines can carry as many passengers as 16 highway lanes, while generating 60 percent less nitrogen oxide and almost no carbon monoxide or particulates. And taking cars off crowded roads actually increases the speed of those that remain more than proportionally, so that in total, vehicles cover more kilometers in less time.[60]

Governments in the U.S. spend roughly $83 billion a year on road-related services—nearly as much as on roads.

Sprawl-abetting cross-subsidies for other forms of infrastructure are also widespread. Many, if not most, local governments also pay for basic services such as sewers and fire stations out of property taxes and other general levies. That amplifies incentives for sprawl. The denser a development, the more people a local fire station, for example, can serve, and the cheaper fire protection becomes per resident. If developers do not pay the full costs they impose on government, sprawl will continue as if it were cheap, societies will end up spending more on infrastructure, and people will again drive more. One solution is to charge developers "impact fees" to pay for the new schools, water mains, and fire departments that come with growth.[61]

Some local governments have begun levying impact fees, but as with road user charges, there is still far to go before full cost recovery becomes universal. In the United States, the use of impact fees first took off in the 1970s in tandem with environmental awareness and resentment of rising property taxes. By the mid-1980s, some 190 localities, mostly in fast-growing Florida and California, had adopted the most usual kind of impact fee, one for sewers. But few of these charges fully covered the costs of new services. Among these, even fewer used a formula that accurately reflected the relationship between cost and location. And most of the country's roughly 1,300 rapid-growth communities did not use impact fees at all.[62]

It makes little sense for societies to leave such cross-subsidies in place even as they struggle with other, costly means to control rush hour traffic jams, air pollution, and oil import dependence. Of course, many factors besides infrastructure pricing, such as zoning and fear of crime, also propel the dispersion of people across the landscape. Elimination of such hidden subsidies for infrastructure, however, would be a good first step toward making towns and cities environmentally sustainable—and easier places to get around in.[63]

Fostering Technologies for Sustainability

One of the most fundamental flaws of today's economies is that they often insulate businesses and consumers from the environmental side effects of their actions. Even though one person's contribution to acid rain or smog harms other people's health and property, there is no practical way for the victims and polluter to meet in court or strike a compromise, especially since some of the victims are not even born yet. As a result, environmental destruction often seems cheap or free to its beneficiaries: in effect, they are cross-subsidized by the people they harm. Government intervention is indispensable to ending this self-destructive pattern.[64]

If traffic police handed out bonuses to people who stopped at red lights rather than ticketing those who did not, they would quickly drive local governments into insolvency. By the same token, any society that tries to subsidize itself all the way to sustainability, paying people not to pollute, will soon bankrupt itself. Taxes and regulations on pollution and resource depletion are ultimately needed to level the economic playing field for environmentally sound ways of living and producing.

That said, targeted subsidies can sometimes play a useful role in protecting the environment—and will always be more popular than taxes and regulations. In late 1992 a 1.5-cent-per-kilowatt-hour tax credit for electricity from wind and biomass sailed through the U.S. Congress with little controversy. Only a few months later, President Clinton's energy tax proposal, which would have handicapped conventional sources by only 0.3 cents more, fell victim to vociferous industry and popular opposition. Subsidies for environmental protection, then, though a second-best policy solution, will likely be useful for decades to come.[65]

Funding specifically for research, development, and commercialization activities for new technologies can also grease the machinery of economic change. Several biases against new technologies in modern economies argue for government intervention. Commercial benefits from the most important scientific discoveries can take decades to materialize and may never accrue to the original researchers. As a result, many businesses, especially small ones, shy away from investing in basic R&D. Basic research, moreover, is only the first step on the difficult road to commercialization. New technologies like wind turbines often have trouble competing with established ones, such as fossil fuel power plants. It is harder for small companies with new technologies to survive price wars or business downturns, to invest in large factories that capture economies of scale, and to gain the confidence of investors and customers. On the other hand, big corporations with large capital investments in the current generation of technology products are often reluctant to innovate.[66]

Targeted government incentives, ideally transitional ones, can help makers of promising and environmentally sound technologies overcome barriers to market entry. At their best, targeted subsidies work with the grain of culture, technology, and economics rather than against it, leveraging small amounts of money into enough technological change that the subsidies themselves become unnecessary. The strength of such subsidies lies not in the brute force of megabucks but in careful design and experimentation. They are more catalytic than coercive.

In practice, however, the track record of R&D subsidies has been poor. One important example of both the strengths and the dangers of targeted commercialization subsidies is provided by the Green Revolution—the combination of grain varieties, pesticides, fertilizers, and irrigation that received active government support in developing countries starting in the 1960s. Though not without serious social and environmental side effects, such as those manifest in India's Gujarat, the Green Revolution did persuade millions of risk-averse farmers to grow food in new, high-yielding ways, which reduced hunger even among rapidly growing populations. The revolution is now largely complete. Yet many of the subsidies that helped spawn it persist, distorting such decisions as when pesticides are worth the costs and health risks.[67]

In a 1985 study, WRI economist Robert Repetto analyzed the effects of pesticide subsidies on farmers' decisions, using data from experimental rice plots in the Philippines. He showed that without subsidies, heavy pesticide doses there were a losing proposition: the additional dose would cost 108 pesos more per hectare than it earned by boosting rice growth. With a 50 percent pesticide subsidy, however, the cost turned into a gain of 434 pesos per hectare. As of the early 1980s, many developing countries, including China, Egypt, and Columbia, used cash payments, tax breaks, and exchange rate controls to cut pesticide prices by 19–89 percent, according to Repetto. Some of those countries have reduced or eliminated pesticide supports, but others have since adopted them. Especially when the financial gains from using chemical inputs closely matches those of alternatives, such as pesticide-resistant crop varieties, subsidies can tip the balance toward practices that, though potentially useful in moderation, also endanger farmers and their land.[68]

Nuclear fission funding has amounted to a permanent subsidy for a new technology, a paradox that hints at failure.

One realm in which subsidies for environmentally important technologies have worked fairly well is energy efficiency. Three of the most successful technologies supported by the U.S. Department of Energy (DOE)—heat-reflecting windows, electronic ballasts for fluorescent lights, and variable-capacity supermarket refrigeration systems—are now saving enough energy to easily justify DOE's entire $425-million efficiency R&D budget.[69]

Though tiny, the $23.7 million public investment in these three technologies was pivotal to their development. In all three cases, it was small companies, which would have had difficulty embarking on such risky research on their own, that vied for the initial grants. Only when their efforts bore fruit did established firms take notice. Most likely, then, it would have taken much longer for the technologies to have developed without government help. The efficient windows, ballasts, and refrigerators already sold will save $8.9 billion in fuel costs over their lifetimes—375 times what DOE spent developing them.[70]

A key circumstance behind these impressive numbers is that with businesses and consumers spending so much on energy—$500 billion per year in the United States alone—one successful energy efficiency R&D grant can quickly save enough money to make up for dozens of failed ones. By contrast, public investments in new ways of producing energy

rather than conserving it have not paid off nearly as well.
Western industrial countries alone spent $52 billion (1995
dollars) on energy R&D between 1990 and 1995. Forty-one
percent of that was devoted to a single technology: traditional nuclear fission. Another 21 percent went for advanced
fission and fusion technologies, which seem forever on the
horizon. Only 9 percent went for renewable energy technologies, whose use is growing rapidly in percentage terms
and which are less polluting and often more labor intensive
to produce and operate than conventional power plants.
Thus the energy sources that are the least polluting, fastest
growing, and the best job creators received the least support.
(See Figure 3.)[71]

The heavy funding for nuclear fission in particular has
amounted to a permanent subsidy for the adoption of a new
technology, a paradox that hints at failure. The global
nuclear market has foundered since the 1970s on high costs
and concern about nuclear accidents and radioactive waste
disposal. In the United States, the last plant order was placed
in 1978 and, along with every other made since 1973, was
eventually canceled. The U.S. government has spent $34 bil-
lion (1995 dollars) on fission R&D since 1948; despite this
and other subsidies, only 1 in 50 American utility executives
would now consider buying the technology, according to a
recent survey. Worldwide, nuclear power generation seems
set to decline early in the new century as utilities decom-
mission existing plants.[72]

Funding for renewable energy research has met with its
share of failures too. DOE, for example, has sunk $1.4 billion
over the last 20 years into the development of a solar "tower
of power": an army of 2,000 computer-controlled mirrors
arrayed in the Mojave Desert, all bouncing sunlight toward
a steam generator at the tip of a 100-meter tower. The technology may find a place in the country's energy mix some-
day, but it will probably have trouble competing with sim-
pler rooftop solar cells, which can be mass-produced more
cheaply and exploit one of sunlight's great advantages as an
energy source: that it is naturally dispersed. Windpower

Energy R&D Funding Priorities Versus Trends in Commercial Use, Western Industrial Countries, 1990–95

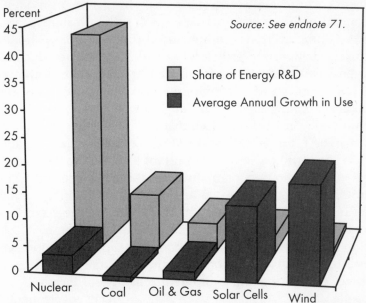

Source: See endnote 71.

☐ Share of Energy R&D
■ Average Annual Growth in Use

research has suffered from a similar top-down mentality. Most publicly funded wind research in Germany, Sweden, the United States, and elsewhere has been performed by agencies and aerospace giants culturally predisposed toward pursuing technical sophistication rather than practicality. Their prototypes have usually been neither reliable nor commercially viable.[73]

People working at the grassroots level, who have less money but a better sense of what people can use, have often had more success in catalyzing change. A U.S.-based non-profit called Enersol, founded by a former nuclear and coal plant engineer, has parlayed modest grants from the World Bank, the Rockefeller Foundation, and other donors into the creation of a nearly self-sustaining solar industry in the Dominican Republic.[74]

Enersol's customers are rural peasants who have no access to the national electricity grid. The nonprofit does not pay for the imported solar panels, but instead has established a revolving loan fund that lets buyers spread payments over several years. The subsidy in this case is modest: some funding to train marketers and system installers, and the willingness to risk losing part of the seed money should buyers default. Nevertheless, the leverage it provides has been tremendous. By 1993, it had brought solar power to 4,000 families and created local employment. Other organizations are now copying this approach in China, Honduras, Indonesia, Sri Lanka, and Zimbabwe.[75]

These forays into technology commercialization and development hold several important lessons. The first is that building expiration dates into subsidies for specific technologies may be warranted to guard against their becoming entrenched despite failure or obsolescence. The second is that the bottom-up approach to technology commercialization typically works better than the top-down approach because it tends to be more responsive to commercial imperatives such as making equipment reliable and meeting customer needs. The last lesson is that, given governments' generally poor track record in picking winners, it may often make more sense to favor broad-gauge subsidies, such as the U.S. tax credit for electricity generation from wind and biomass, over R&D. By focusing more on results, governments can lessen the risk of subsidizing failures, and leave it to the market to pick winners.

Tellingly, the world's most successful windpower industries have arisen in countries where governments have spent little on R&D, instead favoring across-the-board production and investment incentives. Denmark, for example, instituted subsidies for wind turbine investment and power generation in 1979, leaving technology choice to turbine buyers. It retired the investment credit in 1989 after advances had driven prices down and pushed installed capacity from next to nothing to nearly 300 megawatts. And the industry continued to thrive.[76]

More recently, Denmark helped India spark a wind revolution of its own. Inspired by a demonstration wind farm built by the Danish foreign aid agency, and spurred by tax breaks from the Indian government, local companies jumped into the wind business. At first they imported most of their components, but over time they cut costs and increased domestic value added by drawing on the country's own manufacturing strength. By 1995 the Indian wind industry had created hundreds of new jobs and had catapulted to second in the world in annual capacity additions. The striking contrast with India's stagnant, problem-plagued domestic nuclear program suggests that wind technology is easily a better fit for that economy.[77]

Broad-gauge subsidies for pollution control are common in many countries. Like all subsidies for environmental protection, they have the advantage of being politically robust, but are less effective than direct regulation and taxation of pollution. After all, they make activities that do still pollute, if modestly, seem artificially cheap. Brazil, India, Mexico, and most western industrial nations and former Eastern bloc countries offer tax breaks or accelerated depreciation (which allows companies to defer some taxes to later years) for pollution control investments such as smokestack scrubbers and water treatment plants. In one important variation, Poland uses pollution taxes rather than general revenues to fund its investment subsidies.[78]

The Netherlands has developed pollution control incentives perhaps to the fullest. Its tax breaks apply specifically to purchases of 400 or so technologies officially listed as cutting-edge, from devices for recycling concrete to machines that generate ozone for use as a chlorine-free bleaching agent in papermaking. When these become commonplace, they get bumped off the list by newer entries, thus creating a steady prod for industry to push the technological envelope. In another path-breaking step, the Dutch government now grants complete tax exemption for mutual funds that invest in green projects such as wind farms and pollution control R&D.[79]

Though such stories offer some hope, all environmentally friendly technologies face an uphill battle. Conventional technologies like nuclear power often appear falsely cheap because the environmental costs and risks they impose on the rest of society are masked. And many receive much larger subsidies, giving them an unfair market advantage twice over. Only if societies right both of these imbalances will they be able to create more winners like the solar cell retailers in the Dominican Republic and wind turbine manufacturers in India in the numbers needed to achieve environmental sustainability. A direct confrontation with many established interests cannot be avoided.

Political Obstacles to Policy Reform

U.S. Senator Mark O. Hatfield is one of the world's powerful men. In 1995, he ascended to the chairmanship of the U.S. Senate's Appropriations Committee, which, along with its counterpart in the House of Representatives, holds the purse strings of the U.S. government. As a senior member of the committee and as a representative of the timber-rich state of Oregon, he has long, and successfully, pushed the Forest Service to sell more timber than independent scientists and the agency itself have recommended. Two of Hatfield's most important constituencies are the loggers and mill workers who depend on public timber for their living, and the timber companies, which gave more money to him than to any other member of Congress between 1989 and 1994. The high logging rates may have served his constituents in the short term, but they have also forced more below-cost timber sales nationwide, endangering species such as the spotted owl and exhausting the very resource on which the industry depends.[80]

As Chief Minister of the Malaysian state of Sarawak and its Minister of Forests, Tan Sri Datuk Patinggi Abdul Taib bin Mahmud is another of the world's powerful men. He and his

POLITICAL OBSTACLES TO POLICY REFORM

uncle, the former Chief Minister, hold half the state's timber concessions, and his political allies hold others. In his dual role as regulator and timber magnate, Taib has permitted and benefited from logging at a pace that will exhaust the state's commercial wood supplies within a decade.[81]

Hatfield and Taib are living proof that when it comes to subsidies, policy and politics are tightly intertwined. Whatever its purpose, a subsidy calls into being a well-defined, self-aware group of beneficiaries. The subsidized and the subsidizers come naturally to support one another, in a resilient feedback loop. Policymakers use the force of law to hold up their end of the political bargain; recipients use the power of votes, campaign contributions, family connections, or even bribes to deliver on theirs. Sometimes, as in Sarawak, the two groups are the same.

Some of the best-studied instances of the symbiosis between subsidies and one form of influence-peddling—corruption—are occurring in the Asia-Pacific region, the world's major supplier of tropical timber, a resource most inviting of political manipulation. Two characteristic features stand out in such examples. First, the recipients of the cheap extraction rights are few. In Indonesia, for example, there are 584 logging concessions, owned by roughly 50 conglomerates, which appear in turn to be controlled by as few as 15 business figures, including several billionaires.[82]

Second, relations between politicians, military officers, and logging tycoons seem complex and close. According to local environmentalists, three key figures are engineering much of the logging of the Philippine island of Palawan in the 1990s: the Speaker of the House of Representatives, who represents part of the province; the principal shareholder in the province's two biggest logging firms; and the director of the Palawan Philippines National Police. Local environmentalists have reported seeing military escorts for trucks carrying illegally cut logs; the Speaker, meanwhile, is widely understood to be "involved in everything" that happens in Palawan. Though the exact relationships between these figures are not public, they are known to be friends, and it seems likely that all share in the profits from cheap and poorly enforced timber concessions.[83]

Logging-related irregularities are on the rise in other parts of the world as well. In a textbook case of cowboy economics, as Asian companies exhaust timber supplies at home, they are spreading to new countries throughout the tropics, bringing along their old ways of doing business. Allegations of bribery have dogged Indonesian and especially Malaysian companies as they have pressed for entry into timber-rich Brazil, Papua New Guinea, the Solomon Islands, and Suriname on terms that are favorable to themselves but potentially catastrophic for the forests' traditional owners.[84]

Though corruption is a stranger to no country, it tends to influence policy less in industrial democracies than do more above-board means of pressure. The problem of legal influence-peddling is perhaps greatest in the United States in terms of the amount of money changing hands. There, candidates for Congress and the presidency spent $1.6 billion campaigning in 1996, according to preliminary estimates—most of it raised from monied interests with their own agendas. Though this is a huge sum to spend on electing fewer than 500 people, it is trivial compared with the roughly $1.6 trillion at stake each year in federal spending and tax decisions. Ten-thousand-dollar or even million-dollar donations may make politicians' mouths water, but they are peanuts for large corporations, and excellent investments even if they only sway legislators occasionally. Carl Mayer, a politician in Princeton, New Jersey, may not have stretched the truth much when he told a reporter that "giving money to politicians is the best return on an investment... in the entire free world." This is what makes campaign contributions such a stubborn impediment to subsidy reform.[85]

It is politics, and not sound policy, that best explains the remarkable resilience of outmoded resource regimes in the United States. Between 1993 and mid-1996, oil and gas companies gave $10.3 million to protect special tax breaks worth roughly $4 billion over the same period. Timber lobbies donated $2.3 million in an effort to keep the subsidized timber coming. Mining firms handed out $1.9 million to members of Congress to fend off royalty charges on public hardrock minerals, something they have succeeded in doing since 1872. Ranching interests contributed too, in order to keep federal grazing fees low, as they have been since 1906. (Collectively, executives in these companies probably donated similar amounts as individuals, but this is harder to track.) And almost all succeeded in keeping their subsidies in place, despite historic proposals for grazing and mining reform by then newly appointed Interior Secretary, Bruce Babbitt. (During the same period, environmental groups gave only $1.6 million.) Illustrating the economics of campaign donations, the Cyprus Amax Minerals company gave $308,848 to members of Congress, a hefty sum, but only one ten-thousandth of the $3 billion in gross income it stood to gain from a pending claim in Colorado—as long as the 1872 Mining Law remained intact.[86]

In Germany, hard coal unions represent 1 in 300 workers, yet are influential enough to protect $73,000-per-person subsidies.

It is hard to prove that these checks buy legislators' votes. But people would not give the money, and in such strategic ways, if they did not think it worthwhile. Candidates' dependence on such donations—and thus, their vulnerability to industry pressure—is growing steadily. In the case of American resource-based industries, lobbies have usually focused their efforts on the Senate, where it is easier for legislative minorities to obstruct progress, and where lightly populated, resource-rich states have disproportionate clout.[87]

The agricultural company Archer Daniels Midland (ADM) is one of the largest subsidy recipients in the United States, and, probably not coincidentally, one of the largest contributors to both major political parties over the last 30 years. In 1979, Senator Robert Dole sponsored a bill creating a tax break for the production of ethanol. It is a fuel that, at least when distilled from corn, carries questionable environmental credentials since about as much energy goes into making it as is released by burning it, according to several studies. Still, the tax break became law, and was generous enough to create a new industry overnight. The subsidy, now worth 14 cents a liter (54 cents a gallon) has cost the government $6.3 billion since 1983, much of that going to ADM, which holds half the market. Dole has since received more than $255,000 from ADM. More recently Presidents George Bush and Bill Clinton each received donations of $100,000 or more just days before advancing a regulation effectively requiring some ethanol in a tenth of the gasoline sold in the United States—a rule since overturned in court.[88]

Completely removing money from politics (which is perhaps impossible in a free society) would weaken the political advantage of subsidy beneficiaries, but not eliminate it. Subsidy policies and politics are usually asymmetric: there are a few big winners and a lot of small losers. With more at stake, individual subsidy recipients are more apt to organize to defend their interests than the taxpayers and consumers who foot the bill. Thus democracy at its best is still intrinsically vulnerable to distortions by special interests.[89]

In Germany, hard coal union locals now represent 1 in 300 workers, yet are influential enough within the Social Democratic Party to protect $73,000-per-person subsidies that, if granted to all of the labor force, would quickly bankrupt the country. In the Philippines, Venezuela, and other developing countries, riots and street protests have greeted past attempts to cut the gasoline subsidies that are popular among the middle and upper classes. Another factor, fear of unrest among the urban poor, no doubt motivates the suppression of food prices in many developing countries, even when it hurts poor rural farmers.[90]

Not surprisingly, corruption, campaign donation dependence, and special interest politics tend to hurt economies as well as the environment. As these forces strengthen their hold on policymaking, tax and expenditure decisions tend increasingly to serve minority interests at the expense of society as a whole. Of the various methods of influence, corruption costs societies the most. Demands for bribes at every turn can make doing business a slow and unpredictable travail for investors. Recent statistical surveys across dozens of countries have confirmed that both power concentration and corruption correlate with lower investment and economic growth. Nigeria provides one extreme example of this relationship. On the 1996 Corruption Index, compiled by the Berlin-based Trans-parency International, it scored 0.7 out of a possible 10.0, ranking it most corrupt among 54 countries. Not surprisingly, Nigeria's society and economy are also in shambles. The wealth flowing in from oil production is concentrating in the hands of a powerful elite while many Nigerians, including the late Ken Saro-Wiwa's Ogoni people, who live near oil reserves, are losing out.[91]

Though the importance of making government more equitably accountable to all the governed is widely understood, probably few people appreciate the full spectrum of benefits that such a change would bring. Political reforms would, one hopes, help governments earn public confidence. But they could also energize economic development in many countries, such as Nigeria. And without them, it will be nearly impossible to reform many environmentally destructive subsidies.

Subsidy Reform for Sustainable Development

Worldwide, scattered subsidy reforms have occurred over the last decade. Fiscal rather than environmental concerns have motivated most of them. The subsidy cutoffs following the collapse of communism in the former Eastern bloc are a prime example. Whatever has propelled them, the countries that have taken the first steps and, sometimes, missteps toward reform have offered the rest of the world valuable lessons on how best they too should proceed. That said, it is clear that many subsidies are as politically entrenched as ever. Clearly, comprehensive subsidy reform is vital to making modern economies more equitable and sustainable.

The conclusions that arise from applying the principles of good subsidy policy in Table 2 (page 15) to the subsidies in place today can be distilled down to a few fundamental recommendations: withdraw almost all subsidies that perpetuate the cowboy economy; phase out protectionist subsidies that are now or will soon become, like dikes against a rising sea, unnecessary, ineffective, or too costly; target with precision what are now shotgun subsidies, or completely replace them with other methods of helping the poor; pass the costs of infrastructure and related services back to their users in order to slow sprawl; and favor broad-gauged incentives and bottom-up approaches to speed the development of environmentally beneficial technologies. (See Table 3.)

Reform would make subsidies more useful, eliminate most of the $500 billion or more a year in direct costs to taxpayers and consumers, and help the environment. Bringing down taxes and prices would also reduce the penalties for work and investment that taxes create. At the same time, farmers, companies, and consumers would begin to reduce pollution and use resources such as water and energy more efficiently. Unsustainable and polluting industries, from coal mining to virgin papermaking, would lose some of their artificial market advantage over more sustainable competitors such as solar panel makers and paper recyclers. The sooner reform began, the more orderly it could be, and the less pain would result from dislocation of workers in losing industries. To the extent that low-income people would lose out from higher prices for water and energy, they would be compensated by new, more efficient subsidies aimed directly at them.

Worldwide, there have already been halting move-

TABLE 3

Subsidies for Activities with Harmful Environmental Side Effects: Critiques and Remedies

Avowed Intent	Examples	Effects	How To Improve
Stimulating economic growth	Sales of timber, minerals, and land, sometimes claimed by indigenous peoples, usually at below-market prices; tax breaks for forest clearance	Usually slow economic growth; often harm traditional resource owners; cause massive environmental damage; reduce revenues	Give traditional users more control over resources; sell resources at market rates; use savings to cut other taxes or fund public investment
Protecting consumers from import dependence; protecting jobs in resource-based industries	Subsidies in most industrial countries for crop production, ranching, fishing, logging, or fossil fuel production	Often fail to enhance national security or stem job losses; hurt workers in countries unable to offer subsidies; cost taxpayers and environment	Convert subsidies for small operators to welfare; phase out where ineffective or too costly
Reducing the cost of living, especially for the poor	Subsidies for water, electricity, and fuels	Waste money because they usually benefit the poor least; hinder efficiency and renewable energy use	Offer "lifeline" rates or fuel coupons to poor customers; expand access; fund alternatives such as solar panels
Funding infrastructure and related services out of general revenues	Failure to charge drivers for full costs of roads and traffic management	Contribute to road congestion, sprawl, pollution, and oil import dependence	Pass full costs of infrastructure to its users
Supporting technological change	Subsidies for irrigation, pesticides, and fertilizers in developing countries; support for nuclear R&D	Often continue operating after transition has been achieved or has failed, imposing unnecessary fiscal and environmental costs	Halt for mature or failed technologies; subsidize use of environmentally friendly ones, but favor broad-gauged over selective subsidies

Source: Worldwatch Institute.

ments in the direction of reform. In 1988, Brazil ended the generous investment tax credits it had once offered to ranchers and farmers who cleared land in the Amazon; officials there believe this change contributed to the temporary deforestation slowdown that began at that time. The U.S. Congress has yet to reform the 1872 Mining Law, but it has placed a temporary moratorium on new mineral claims on public lands every year since 1994. And although most developing countries still sell timber far too cheaply, many have learned to bargain harder over mineral concessions during the last few decades. Some too, like Indonesia, have cut agrichemical subsidies since the mid-1980s partly in response to falling revenues from oil exports or the tightening vise of overseas debt, while encouraging the use of natural predators to control crop pests. And following the collapse of communism in the former Eastern bloc, the prices that businesses there pay for agrichemicals and fuel have shot up toward world levels. This has caused fertilizer and energy use to plummet, and spurred jolting economic contraction.[92]

Expenditures aimed specifically at protecting resource-based jobs have lately drawn more fire from budget cutters, perhaps because they make more obvious targets than revenues forgone through low taxes, prices, or royalties. When Belgium, France, Japan, Spain, and the United Kingdom eliminated or radically reduced coal subsidies, their combined output fell by half between 1986 and 1995. The imported coal that has replaced some of this output has in general contained less sulfur and ash, and its mining has entailed less environmental damage. In the United Kingdom, moreover, coal consumption has also fallen, as natural gas from the North Sea has grabbed market share. As a result, carbon emissions have declined there during the 1990s even as the economy has expanded—a rare divergence.[93]

Many subsidy cuts have been far from painless, however. In the United Kingdom—where the coal cutback of 27.5 million tons (48 percent) in three years was by far the largest and the most rapid—social ills such as high unemployment and drug abuse have struck many former coal towns. Joblessness and discontent are now rising in Russian farm regions as well in the wake of the rapid market reforms. These tribulations dramatize both the seriousness of the trade-offs that policymakers sometimes face in deciding on subsidy reductions and the importance of trying to mitigate their effects.[94]

Though British Coal offered severance packages and some retraining, perhaps inevitably these have been inadequate to the formidable task of engineering a wholesale transformation of the job bases of dozens of local economies in just three years. Mine-closing programs in continental Europe have often been slower, more generous, and more flexible. Miners in Baersweiller, Germany, for instance, will receive five years' notice if their pit is to close. In Belgian Flanders, the gradual mine closure program was once temporarily halted when local unemployment rose above the national average. Even on the continent, though, serious unemployment has often resulted from mine closings, showing that there is usually no easy way out.[95]

The choices in coal policy are unusually tough because there is no getting around the fact that coal use is a major source of greenhouse gases and other pollutants; but in some resource-based industries it is easier to reduce environmental harm while protecting jobs. The European Union took advantage of the maneuvering room in agricultural policy in 1993 when it decreased guaranteed prices for major crops and instituted flat per-hectare payments. In 1996, the United States leapfrogged the European Union in this direction by completely abolishing price guarantees for most crops in favor of fixed payments based on farmers' past production levels. (Growers of sugar, tobacco, and a few other crops escaped reform.) Both of these "decouplings" are intended to support farmers' incomes while ending the market manipulations that have burdened farmers with complex regulations and encouraged overproduction and environmentally destructive farming.[96]

Remarkably, New Zealand almost completely eliminated its farming supports in the mid-1980s—partly at the
prompting of farmers themselves, through the agency of the
national Federated Farmers group. The move was part of a
broader government effort to cut subsidies that had crept
into many sectors of the economy over several decades,
leading to high taxes and inflation that hurt farmers at least
as much as other workers. After some difficult years of
adjustment, during which the government wrote off many
bad loans to farmers, the agricultural sector became much
more efficient, and rebounded. Interestingly, New Zealand is
now one of the few industrial countries where the number
of farmers is rising.[97]

As with subsidies for producers, many subsidies for
consumers remain in place worldwide, though here too
some countries offer good examples for others to follow. The
U.S. government, for example, targets heating bill assistance
at poor households, though in modest amounts, in order to
hold down costs and minimize the subsidy-induced incentive for energy use and pollution. Such targeting is rarer in
developing countries. In Indonesia, although across-the-
board kerosene subsidies have reduced the cost of living for
most families in the poorest one-fifth of the population, 90
percent of the payments actually benefit people who are better off. If the subsidy were restricted to the neediest recipients, it could give them 10 times the benefit for the same
cost, or the same benefit for one-tenth the cost.[98]

In countries like Indonesia, where governments are
strapped for cash and most economic activity occurs off the
books, identifying and targeting the neediest for subsidization can be a daunting task. But there are proven, cost-effec-
tive ways to sharpen, if not perfect, subsidy focus even in
developing countries. These include targeting particularly
poor neighborhoods and regions, and involving schoolteach-
ers, who know local communities well, in determining
which families are deserving. Sri Lanka used such approaches to distribute "kerosene stamps" among the poorer half of
the population, in order to soften the blow of the 1979 oil

shock. In the same spirit, Sri Lanka, along with at least a dozen developing countries, offers "lifeline" rates for electricity: discounts on the first 20 kilowatt-hours or so used each month, enough to power a couple of light bulbs every evening.[99]

One problem with resource consumption subsidies, no matter how carefully targeted or vital to the poor they are, is that they handicap cleaner alternatives. This is why the U.S. government also offers some funding to help low-income people invest in efficiency upgrades for furnaces and home insulation. In doing so, it lowers the very heating bills it is helping to pay. By the same token, if Sri Lanka and other countries continue to pursue a policy of using cheap energy to mitigate poverty, they will succeed better by subsidizing *all* forms of energy used by the poor that are practical to subsidize. That would include renewable technologies such as solar panels, which are safer and cleaner than kerosene and particularly appropriate in areas not reached by power lines.[100]

To date, the largest subsidies for activities with environmentally beneficial effects—like the largest ones for activities with destructive effects—have been offered to farmers, whom industrial countries have begun to view not just as producers of food, but as potential stewards of the rural landscape. The recent U.S. farm bill, for example, authorized spending $2.2 billion between 1996 and 2002 on a large collection of "agri-environmental" measures, including payments to farmers to keep highly erodible soils, wetlands, and other wildlife habitat out of production. Similar programs have proliferated in the European Union in the 1990s, costing $1.7 billion in 1995 alone.[101]

Such subsidies are more politically viable than taxes and regulations designed to bring about the same environmental benefit. Historically, though, many such programs have fallen short of their full potential because they have often emphasized reducing crop surpluses by idling the most productive, rather than the most fragile or ecologically valuable lands. Moreover, though the funding levels for these programs are impressive, cutting the hundreds of billions of dollars of remaining subsidies for crop *production* would probably help consumers, taxpayers, and the environment much more.[102]

Overall, subsidy reform is a project far from completion. To continue and accelerate progress, policymakers will need to attack entrenched subsidies from several angles at once, from curtailing the influence of monied interests in policymaking to documenting the magnitudes of subsidies. In the area of corruption, which is receiving growing academic scrutiny, several principles have emerged to guide reform. One is that officials who formulate and implement policy should be well salaried, in order to reduce the appeal of bribes. In the Philippines' Department of Environment and Natural Resources, as in many other governments, low pay is one factor that contributes to corruption among timber concession administrators, which the department's own Secretary has admitted is rampant. Adoption and enforcement of strong anti-corruption laws, periodic auditing of officials, and an independent judiciary are also critical; enforcement will never stamp out corruption completely, but it will increase the risks for potential bribe takers. Finally, reducing the discretion of bureaucratic decision-makers and making their actions public—for example by holding competitive, public auctions for resource concessions—will further reduce the appeal of bribery.[103]

Decreasing the influence of money in electoral politics without violating people's right to freedom of expression is another knotty problem. Each western industrial country has adopted its own mix of techniques, choosing from such ingredients as bans on political television advertising, public campaign financing, and limits on political contributions and spending. Probably inevitably, none of these attempted solutions have come close to achieving the ideal of money-free politics; but some have worked better than others. In Canada, for instance, a 1974 package of reforms combining strong spending caps for political parties, disclosure requirements, tax credits for private donations, and direct public financing has had some success. Though by no means perfect, the reforms did limit campaign spending for the most recent federal elections to 80 cents per capita, compared to $6 in the United States. And they do appear to have facilitated the rise of new political parties.[104]

Another basic step supporters of reform can take is simply to measure and document subsidies: it is hard to reform what cannot be seen. Worldwide, governments have little idea of the overall magnitude and effects of the subsidies they offer. In the United States, taxpayer and environmental groups have joined forces to produce the annual "Green Scissors" report, which summarizes the environmental and fiscal arguments against more than a score of federal subsidies. The coalition, its report, and the publicity they have won may have played a crucial role in the recent defeat of several subsidies, such as those for some types of nuclear energy research.[105]

Ultimately, however, it is governments themselves that are best positioned to measure subsidies. But few subsidizing agencies have taken up the challenge, and even fewer have produced results that seem anything more than self-serving. The forest agency of the government of Victoria, Australia, for instance, has generally released accounting data to the public only stingily. In this data, it treats spending on forest maintenance as revenue, based on the argument that it increases the value of a forest; but when forest value falls—when loggers haul out trees—no loss shows up on the expense side. These and other questionable accounting practices make $170 million in annual losses look like only $10 million, according to Andrew Dragun, an economist formerly at LaTrobe University in Melbourne. Similar stories of resistance to disclosure and obfuscation abound almost anywhere governments manage natural resources. Far more useful have been the efforts of the Paris-based, government-funded Organisation for Economic Co-operation and Development (OECD) to measure agriculture and coal subsidies in western industrial countries, and those of the World Bank to gauge energy subsidies in the rest of the world.[106]

Negotiations over trade pacts have provided another pressure point for subsidy reform and political reform. During the protracted 10-year Uruguay Round negotiations that ended with a new General Agreement on Tariffs and Trade (GATT) in 1993, agricultural subsidies were one of the toughest sticking points among industrial countries and between them and poorer ones that could not afford the same protection for their own farmers. Despite New Zealand's example, probably few industrial countries would have agreed to cut their own subsidies without a multilateral agreement guaranteeing that their competitors would too. The final deal, though modest—20 percent cuts in production incentives relative to high late-1980s levels—did at least establish that agriculture subsidies, like other subsidies, are fair game in the international trade arena. The need for data during the negotiations was also what prompted the OECD to begin measuring these subsidies. More recently, U.S. trade representatives have begun to argue that where government corruption is endemic, it favors domestic companies that are willing to pay bribes, over foreign companies, which may be less able to play by local rules. Endemic corruption, they argue, is therefore in effect a government policy that restrains trade and so is subject to discussion under GATT. This assertion has proved particularly controversial in Asia.[107]

International aid institutions, which have too often ended up facilitating shortsighted resource giveaway policies in the past, also need to become stronger allies in the fight for subsidy and political reforms. One key leverage point they should exploit more is the training of the government officials who negotiate concession agreements. A few million dollars spent educating them in the financial, engineering, and environmental complexities of international resource-based industries and the finer points of negotiation can translate into billions more in royalty payments.[108]

Under the rubric of "structural adjustment," both the World Bank and the International Monetary Fund have actually pressed nations struggling to repay past debts to reduce public subsidies. But often they have allowed debtors to cut back the subsidies with the weakest political bases— such as those primarily benefiting the poor—rather than those with the weakest policy rationales. Nevertheless, there are signs that these institutions are beginning to take environmentally destructive subsidies more seriously. In 1996, for example, the Bank conditioned a structural adjustment loan to Papua New Guinea on reforms of the corrupt and loss-laden Forest Authority. After several months of direct resistance, the government finally relented, passing a law to raise prices on forest concessions and include representatives from environmental and indigenous groups on the agency's governing board. But in countries where the Bank's credit is less needed, its influence weakens. In Indonesia, it tried with little success in the late 1980s to convince the Indonesian government to rein in underpricing and overcutting of timber, and, implicitly, the rampant cronyism behind it. The only apparent result was Indonesia's loss of interest in Bank funding for timber projects.[109]

Societies will ultimately need to take steps more fundamental than subsidy reform if they are to attain environmental sustainability. While they will still use subsidies to reward, they will need environmental taxes to penalize, and regulations to restrict. Yet environmentally harmful subsidies have so many strikes against them that reforming them should be an easier step politically. They do little good on their own terms. They hike the cost of government. The resulting higher taxes and prices burden economies. Moreover, these subsidies degrade the environment, further undermining long-term economic prospects.

Citizens and policymakers determined to forge economies that are just and prosperous for generations to come could do little better than to start by withdrawing from the business of paying the polluter. Failure to take this first step would cast doubt on their ability to prevail in the even tougher political fights that lie beyond.

Notes

Some of the references in this paper were obtained on-line from confer-
ences of the Association for Progressive Communications (APC), which in
the United States are maintained and archived by the Institute for Global
Communications in San Francisco.

1. Evsey Gurvich et al., "Impact of Russian Energy Subsidies on Green-
house Gas Emissions," preliminary draft report to OECD Environment
Directorate, Paris, 1995; U.S. Congress, Office of Technology Assessment
(OTA), *Energy Efficiency Technologies for Central and Eastern Europe*
(Washington, D.C.: U.S. Government Printing Office (GPO), 1993).

2. U.S. Congress, Committee on Natural Resources, Subcommittee on
Oversight and Investigations, "Taking from the Taxpayer: Public Subsidies
for Natural Resource Development," Majority Staff Report, Washington,
D.C., 1994; "few hundred square meters" is based on Peter H. Gleick, ed.,
Water in Crisis: A Guide to the World's Fresh Water Resources (New York:
Oxford University Press, 1993); original intent from Charles F. Wilkinson,
Crossing the Next Meridian: Land, Water, and the Future of the West
(Washington, D.C.: Island Press, 1992); Simplot from Edward A. Chadd,
"How Congress Pays Industry—with Federal Tax Dollars—To Deplete and
Destroy the Nation's Natural Resources," *Common Cause*, Fall 1995.

3. Figure of $500 billion is a Worldwatch estimate, based on sources cited
later in text. Figure of $7.5 trillion is a Worldwatch estimate, based on
International Monetary Fund (IMF), *Government Finance Statistics Yearbook
1994* (Washington, D.C., 1994), on IMF, *World Economic Outlook—October
1994* (Washington, D.C., 1994), on Organisation for Economic Co-operation and Development (OECD), *Revenue Statistics of OECD Member Countries
1960–1994* (Paris, 1995), on World Bank, *World Data 1994: World Bank
Indicators on CD-ROM* (electronic database) (Washington, D.C., 1994), and
on Thomas Sterner, "Environmental Tax Reform: Theory, Industrialized
Country Experience, and Relevance in LDCs," Unit for Environmental
Economics, Department of Economics, Gothenburg University,
Gothenburg, Sweden, 1994. It excludes local and regional government rev-
enue in developing countries, but includes non-tax revenue there. For an
analysis of the economic burden of taxation, see Dale W. Jorgenson and
Yun Kun-Young, "The Excess Burden of Taxation in the U.S.," Discussion
Paper No. 1528, Harvard Institute for Economic Research (HIER), Harvard
University, Cambridge, Mass., 1990, as cited in Roger C. Dower and Mary
Beth Zimmerman, *The Right Climate for Carbon Taxes: Creating Economic
Incentives to Protect the Atmosphere* (Washington, D.C.: World Resources
Institute (WRI), 1992).

4. OECD, *Agricultural Policies, Markets and Trade in OECD Countries* (Paris,
1996).

5. Gurvich et al., op. cit. note 1; OECD, *Agricultural Policies, Markets, and*

Trade in the Central and Eastern European Countries, the New Independent States, and China (Paris, 1995); OECD, International Energy Agency (IEA), *Energy Policies of IEA Countries* (Paris, various years); Jamshid Heidarian and Gary Wu, *Power Sector Statistics for Developing Countries, 1987–1991* (World Bank: Washington, D.C., 1994); Christina Olivecrona, "Wind Energy in Denmark," in Robert Gale and Stephan Barg, eds., *Green Budget Reform: An International Casebook of Leading Practices* (London: Earthscan, 1995); India and Dominican Republic from Keith Kozloff and Olatokumbo Shobowale, *Rethinking Development Assistance for Renewable Electricity* (Washington, D.C.: WRI, 1994).

6. Courtney Cuff, Gawain Kripke, and Adam Van de Water, eds., "Green Scissors," Friends of the Earth (FOE), Washington, D.C., 1996; U.S. Department of Agriculture (USDA), "1996 Farm Bill Conservation Provisions," Washington, D.C., 1996.

7. Douglas Koplow, *Federal Energy Subsidies: Energy, Environmental, and Fiscal Impacts* (Washington, D.C.: Alliance to Save Energy, 1993).

8. "Quest for 'Green Gold' Fells One of Earth's Oldest Rain Forests," Associated Press, 7 May 1996.

9. Nicholas Lenssen and Christopher Flavin, "Meltdown," *World Watch*, May/June 1996.

10. For a broad conservative attack on subsidies, see Stephen Moore and Dean Stansel, "Ending Corporate Welfare As We Know It," Policy Analysis No. 225, Cato Institute, Washington, D.C., 1995; on the precedence of other societal values over economic efficiency, see Mark Sagoff, *The Economy of the Earth: Philosophy, Law, and the Environment* (Cambridge, U.K.: University of Cambridge Press, 1988).

11. Kenneth E. Boulding, *Environmental Quality in a Growing Economy* (Baltimore: Johns Hopkins University Press, 1966), excerpted as Kenneth E. Boulding, "The Economics of the Coming Spaceship Earth," in Herman E. Daly and Kenneth N. Townsend, eds., *Valuing the Earth: Economics, Ecology, Ethics* (Cambridge, Mass.: MIT Press, 1993).

12. Wilkinson, op. cit. note 2.

13. Figure of 400 million hectares from ibid.; Juri Peepre, Canadian Parks and Wilderness Society, White Horse, Yukon, private communication, 24 June 1996; Thomas J. Hilliard, "Golden Patents, Empty Pockets: A 19th Century Law Gives Miners Billions, the Public Pennies," Mineral Policy Center (MPC), Washington, D.C., 1994; U.S. Office of Management and Budget (OMB), *Budget of the United States Government, Fiscal Year 1997* (Washington, D.C.: GPO, 1996).

14. U.S. Congress, op. cit. note 2; Canadian grazing subsidies from Peepre, op. cit. note 13, and from John C. Ryan, *Hazardous Handouts: Taxpayer Subsidies to Environmental Degradation*, NEW Report No. 2, Northwest Environment Watch (Seattle: NEW 1995).

15. Quota system from Charles Victor Barber, Nels C. Johnson, and Emmy Hafild, *Breaking the Logjam: Obstacles to Forest Policy Reform in Indonesia and the United States* (Washington, D.C.: WRI, 1994); Randal O'Toole, "Timber Sale Subsidies, But Who Gets Them?" *Different Drummer* (Thoreau Institute, Oak Grove, Oreg.), Spring 1995; Tongass from U.S. Congress, op. cit. note 2; Andrew K. Dragun, "The Subsidization of Logging in Victoria," unpublished paper, LaTrobe University, Melbourne, 1995.

16. Wilkinson, op. cit. note 2; Betty Ballantine and Ian Ballantine, eds., *The Native Americans: An Illustrated History* (Atlanta: Turner Publishing, 1993); Barber et al., op. cit. note 15; Australia from Alan B. Durning and Holly B. Brough, *Taking Stock: Animal Farming and the Environment*, Worldwatch Paper 103 (Washington, D.C.: Worldwatch Institute, July 1991); American West from William E. Riebsame, "Ending the Range Wars?" *Environment*, May 1996.

17. Polling data are based on a sample of 1,000 adults taken in September 1995 by Yankelovich Partners, Inc., Norwalk, Conn., cited in Kate Stewart, Belden & Russonello, Washington, D.C., private communication and printout, 10 September 1996; new settlers from Riebsame, op. cit. note 16; John C. Ryan and Aaron M. Best, "NEW Indicator: Northwest Employment Depends Less on Timber and Mining," press release, NEW, Seattle, 30 November 1994.

18. Theodore Panayotou and Peter S. Ashton, *Not By Timber Alone: Economics and Ecology for Sustaining Tropical Forests* (Washington, D.C.: Island Press, 1992).

19. Figure 1 is based on U.N. Food and Agriculture Organization (FAO), *Forest Products Yearbook* (Rome, various years), on FAO, *Forest Products Electronic Database* (electronic database) (Rome, 1995), on Crissis Vici, FAO, Rome, private communication, 20 August 1996, on *ICSG Copper Bulletin* (International Copper Study Group, Lisbon), May 1996, on Daniel Edelstein, U.S. Geological Survey, Reston, Va., private communication and printout, 7 July 1996, on United Nations (UN), *World Energy Supplies* (New York, various years), on UN, *Yearbook of World Energy Statistics* (New York, 1983), on UN, *Energy Statistics Yearbook* (New York, various years), and on British Petroleum (BP), *BP Statistical Review of World Energy* (electronic database) (London, 1996).

20. Jeffrey D. Sachs and Andrew M. Warner, "Natural Resource Abundance and Economic Growth," Development Discussion Paper No. 517a, Harvard Institute for International Development, Cambridge, Mass., October 1995.

21. Edward A. Gargan, "Family Ties That Bind Growth: Corruption Is But

One Obstacle to Indonesia's Future," *New York Times*, 9 April 1996; Barber et al., op. cit. note 15; Robert Repetto, *The Forest for the Trees? Government Policies and the Misuse of Forest Resources* (Washington, D.C.: WRI, 1988).

22. David N. Smith and Louis T. Wells, Jr., *Negotiating Third-World Mineral Agreements: Promises as Prologue* (Cambridge, Mass.: Ballinger, 1975); figure of 85 percent from Barber et al., op. cit. note 15; new countries from David Smith, Harvard Law School, Cambridge, Mass., private communication, 13 August 1996.

23. A.H. Gelb, *Oil Windfalls: Blessing or Curse?* (New York: Oxford University Press, 1988); Saudi windfall is a Worldwatch estimate based on oil prices and production from BP, op. cit. note 19; Saudi economic drop based on Robert Summers and Alan Heston, "The Penn World Table (Mark 5): An Expanded Set of International Comparisons, 1950–1988," *Quarterly Journal of Economics*, May 1991, and electronic database.

24. Gelb, op. cit. note 23.

25. Ibid.

26. Ecuador and Nigeria from Aaron Sachs, *Eco-Justice: Linking Human Rights and the Environment*, Worldwatch Paper 127 (Washington, D.C.: Worldwatch Institute, December 1995); Guyana from Fred Pearce, "Caught in the Gold Rush," *New Scientist*, 11 May 1996; Helen Rosenbaum and Michael Krockenberger, "Report on the Impacts of the Ok Tedi Mine in Papua New Guinea," Australian Conservation Foundation (ACF), Fitzroy, Victoria, Australia, 1993; Botswana from Durning and Brough, op. cit. note 16; Brazil and Côte d'Ivoire from Repetto, op. cit. note 21; Greenpeace International, "Logging In Solomon Islands Takes Its Toll," Greenpeace Briefing, Rome, undated, APC conference <rainfor.general>, 12 December 1995.

27. Barber et al., op. cit. note 15.

28. Smith and Wells, op. cit. note 22.

29. Oil reserves from BP, op. cit. note 19; size of European Union subsidies from OECD, op. cit. note 4.

30. Income doubling from Summers and Heston, op. cit. note 23.

31. Coal policies from OECD, *Energy Policies*, op. cit. note 5, and from Gurvich et al., op. cit. note 1.

32. Falling farm count from U.S. Department of Commerce (DOC), Bureau of the Census, *Historical Statistics of the United States: Colonial Times to 1970* (Washington, D.C.: GPO, 1975), and from DOC, Bureau of the Census, *Statistical Abstract of the United States 1994* (Washington, D.C., 1994); subsidy distribution from Paul Faeth, *Growing Green: Enhancing the Economic and Environmental Performance of U.S. Agriculture* (Washington, D.C.: WRI, 1995). Subsidy shares total more than 100 percent because of rounding.

33. Réda Soufi and Mark Tuddenham, "The Reform of European Union Common Agricultural Policy," in Gale and Barg, op. cit. note 5; USDA, *Production, Supply, and Demand View* (electronic database) (Washington, D.C., 1996).

34. OECD, op. cit. note 4. Figures exclude Turkey.

35. Brian Chamberlin, *Farming and Subsidies: Debunking the Myths* (Pukekohe, New Zealand: Euroa Farms, 1996).

36. Effects in the United States from Faeth, op. cit. note 32; effects in Western Europe from C. Ford Runge, "The Environmental Impacts of Agricultural and Forest Subsidies," in OECD, *Subsidies and Environment: Exploring the Linkages* (Paris, 1996); effects in the former Eastern bloc from Sergei Bobyliev and Bo Libert, "Prospects for Agricultural and Environmental Policy Integration in Russia," in OECD, *Agriculture and the Environment in the Transition to a Market Economy* (Paris, 1994); effects in developing countries from Kevin Watkins and Michael Windfuhr, "Agriculture in the Uruguay Round: Implications for Sustainable Development in Developing Countries," WWF International Discussion Paper, World Wide Fund For Nature, Gland, Switzerland, 1995.

37. Rory McLeod, "Market Access Issues for the New Zealand Seafood Trade," New Zealand Fishing Industry Board, Wellington, 1996; figure of $54 billion from FAO, *Marine Fisheries and the Law of the Sea: A Decade of Change*, FAO Fisheries Circular No. 853 (Rome, 1993); "has lowered" is a Worldwatch estimate based on ibid., and on Vladimir Fedoremko, Fisheries Attaché, Embassy of the Russian Federation, Washington, D.C., private communication, 28 October 1996; Peter Weber, *Net Loss: Fish, Jobs, and the Marine Environment*, Worldwatch Paper 120 (Washington, D.C.: Worldwatch Institute, July 1994).

38. On the competitive advantages of large companies, see John Kenneth Galbraith, *Economics and the Public Purpose* (Boston: Houghton Mifflin, 1973).

39. Barber et al., op. cit. note 15.

40. Tax breaks from U.S. Congress, op. cit. note 2; market share from U.S. Department of Energy (DOE), Energy Information Administration (EIA), *Monthly Energy Review—August 1996* (Washington, D.C.: GPO, 1996).

41. Figure 2 and figures in text are based on OECD, IEA, *Coal Prospects and Policies in IEA Countries—1987 Review* (Paris, 1988), on OECD, *Energy Policies*, op. cit. note 5, and on OECD, IEA, *Coal Information* (Paris, various years), with costs converted using a 1995 exchange rate.

42. Western countries are from OECD, *Energy Policies*, op. cit. note 5, using a 1995 exchange rate; Russian total is from Gurvich et al., op. cit. note 1, and uses a 1994 exchange rate.

43. Runge, op. cit. note 36; German commitment from Christopher Flavin and Odil Tunali, *Climate of Hope: New Strategies for Stabilizing the World's Climate*, Worldwatch Paper 130 (Washington, D.C.: Worldwatch Institute, June 1996).

44. Bjorn Larsen and Anwar Shah, "World Fossil Fuel Subsidies and Global Carbon Emissions," background paper for *World Development Report 1992*, World Bank, Washington, D.C., 1992; figure of 15 nations based on U.N. Development Programme, *Human Development Report 1994* (New York: Oxford University Press, 1994).

45. Relationship between income and expenditures on energy in Indonesia and other developing countries from Christine Kerr and Leslie Citroen, "Household Expenditures on Infrastructure Services," background paper for *World Development Report 1994*, World Bank, Washington, D.C., undated; relationship in United States from James Poterba, "Tax Policy to Combat Global Warming: On Designing a Carbon Tax," in Rudiger Dornbusch and James Poterba, eds., *Global Warming: Economic Policy Responses* (Cambridge, Mass.: MIT Press, 1991); relationship in Western Europe from Mark Pearson, "Equity Issues and Carbon Taxes," in OECD, *Climate Change: Designing a Practical Tax System* (Paris, 1993).

46. Bjorn Larsen and Anwar Shah, "Global Climate Change, Energy Subsidies and National Carbon Taxes," in Lans Bovenberg and Sijbren Cnossen, eds., *Public Economics and the Environment in an Imperfect World* (Boston: Kluwer Academic Press, 1995); energy waste from U.S. Congress, op. cit. note 1; subsidy developments since 1991 from Gurvich et al., op. cit. note 1.

47. Larsen and Shah, op. cit. note 46; World Bank, Energy Development Division, *Review of Electricity Tariffs in Developing Countries During the 1980s*, Industry and Energy Department Working Paper, Energy Series Paper No. 32 (Washington, D.C., 1990); figure of $46 billion from Gregory K. Ingraham and Marianne Fay, "Valuing Infrastructure Stocks and Gains from Improved Performance," background paper for *World Development Report 1994*, World Bank, 1994; Brazil from Gunter Schramm, "Operationalizing Efficiency Criteria in Energy Pricing Policy," in Corazón Morales Siddayao, ed., *Criteria for Energy Pricing Policy* (London: Graham & Trotman, 1985), cited in Mark Kosmo, *Money to Burn? The High Costs of Energy Subsidies* (Washington, D.C.: WRI, 1987).

48. Giancarlo Tosato, "Environmental Implications of Support to the Electric Sector in Italy: A Case Study," Preliminary Draft Report to OECD

Environment Directorate, Paris, 1995, cited in Laurie Michaelis, "The Environmental Implications of Energy and Transport Subsidies," in OECD, *Subsidies and Environment*, op. cit. note 36; tax breaks from Koplow, op. cit. note 7; loss on power sales from DOE, EIA, *Federal Energy Subsidies: Direct and Indirect Interventions in Energy Markets* (Washington, D.C.: GPO, 1992).

49. U.S. Congress, op. cit. note 2; Tim Fisher, ACF, Fitzroy, Victoria, Australia, private communication, 8 July 1996; Bobyliev and Libert, op. cit. note 36; figure of $13 billion from Ingraham and Fay, op. cit. note 47.

50. U.S. Congress, op. cit. note 2.

51. Kosmo, op. cit. note 47.

52. Gurvich et al., op. cit. note 1; Sandra Postel, *Last Oasis: Facing Water Scarcity* (New York: W.W. Norton, 1992).

53. Doug Koplow, "Energy Subsidies and the Environment," in OECD, *Subsidies and Environment*, op. cit. note 36; aluminum subsidies in the Northwest from Douglas Koplow, "Federal Energy Subsidies and Recycling: A Case Study," *Resource Recycling*, November 1994; worldwide pattern from Jennifer S. Gitlitz, "The Relationship Between Primary Aluminum Production and the Damming of World Rivers," International Rivers Network, Berkeley, Calif., 1993.

54. Subsidy distribution from World Bank, *World Development Report 1994* (Washington, D.C., 1994).

55. Figures of one and two billion from ibid.; disease figure is computed in disability-adjusted life years, a unit that measures both disability and loss of years of life, and is from World Bank, *World Development Report 1993* (Washington, D.C., 1993); price disparities from Kerr and Citroen, op. cit. note 45.

56. Robert Repetto, *Skimming the Water: Rent-Seeking and the Performance of Public Irrigation Systems* (Washington, D.C.: WRI, 1986); Bela Bhatia, "Lush Fields and Parched Throats: The Political Economy of Groundwater in Gujarat," World Institute for Development Economics Research, Helsinki, 1992.

57. France figure from Michaelis, op. cit. note 48; developing countries from V. Swaroop, "The Public Finances of Infrastructure: Issues and Options," *World Development*, Vol. 22, No. 12, 1994; U.S. figure is from U.S. Department of Transportation (DOT), Federal Highway Administration, *Highway Statistics 1994* (Washington, D.C., 1995) and includes road user fees designated for non-road uses on the revenue side.

58. Figure of $20 billion from "Transportation Sector Subsidies: U.S. Case Study," prepared for U.S. Environmental Protection Agency, DRI/McGraw-

Hill, Lexington, Mass., 1994; mass transit coupons from Douglas Shoup, University of California at Los Angeles, Los Angeles, private communication, 6 September 1996; James J. MacKenzie, Roger C. Dower, and Donald D.T. Chen, *The Going Rate: What it Really Costs to Drive* (Washington, D.C.: WRI, 1992); U.S. road spending from DOT, op. cit. note 57; price rise is a Worldwatch estimate based on a motor fuel usage rate from ibid.

59. DOE, op. cit. note 40; figure of $100 billion from MacKenzie et al., op. cit. note 58; Ted Bardacke, "Bangkok May Ban New Cars Until 2001," *Financial Times*, 8 July 1996; figure of $2.3 billion from Gordon Fairclough, "Motion Sickness: Little Relief in Sight for Bangkok's Traffic Ailments," *Far Eastern Economic Review*, 15 February 1996.

60. Marcia D. Lowe, *Back on Track: The Global Rail Revival*, Worldwatch Paper 118 (Washington, D.C.: Worldwatch Institute, April 1994); Richard Arnot and Kenneth Small, "The Economics of Traffic Congestion," *American Scientist*, September-October 1994.

61. James E. Frank, "The Costs of Alternative Patterns of Development," Urban Land Institute, Washington, D.C., 1989.

62. James E. Frank and Paul B. Downing, "Patterns of Impact Fee Use," in Arthur C. Nelson, ed., *Development Impact Fees: Policy Rationale, Practice, Theory, and Issues* (Chicago: Planners Press, 1988).

63. Marcia Lowe, *Shaping Cities: The Environmental and Human Dimensions*, Worldwatch Paper 105 (Washington, D.C.: Worldwatch Institute, October 1991).

64. A.C. Pigou, *The Economics of Welfare* (New York: AMS Press, 1978); R.H. Coase, "The Problem of Social Cost," *Journal of Law and Economics*, October 1960.

65. Frank Muller, "Tax Credits and the Development of Renewable Energy in California," in Gale and Barg, op. cit. note 5.

66. "Economic and Social Significance of Scientific and Engineering Research," in National Science Board, *Science & Engineering Indicators—1996* (Washington, D.C.: GPO, 1996).

67. Edward C. Wolf, *Beyond the Green Revolution: New Approaches for Third World Agriculture*, Worldwatch Paper 73 (Washington, D.C.: Worldwatch Institute, October 1986); continuing fertilizer subsidies from Sanjeev Gupta, Kenneth Miranda, and Ian Parry, "Public Expenditure Policy and the Environment: A Review and Synthesis," IMF Working Paper, IMF, Washington, D.C., 1993; continuing pesticide subsidies from Jumanah Farah, "Pesticide Policies in Developing Countries: Do They Encourage Excessive Use?" World Bank Discussion Paper 238, World Bank, Washington, D.C., 1994.

68. Robert Repetto, *Paying the Price: Pesticide Subsidies in Developing Countries* (Washington, D.C.: WRI, 1985); Farah, op. cit. note 67.

69. Howard Geller and Scott McGaraghan, "Successful Government-Industry Partnership: The U.S. Department of Energy's Role in Advancing Energy-efficient Technologies," American Council for an Energy-Efficient Economy, Washington, D.C., 1996.

70. Ibid.

71. Ibid.; Figure 3 is based on BP, op. cit. note 19, and on OECD, *Energy Policies*, op. cit. note 5, with wind growth statistics from Paul Gipe, Paul Gipe & Associates, Tehachapi, Calif., private communication, 4 September 1996, and solar growth statistics from Bill Murray, Strategies Unlimited, Mountain View, Calif., private communication, 10 September 1996. Growth figure for solar cells is based on domestic sales of solar cells, not electricity generated.

72. Lenssen and Flavin, op. cit. note 9; U.S. subsidy total is based on Fred J. Sissine, "Energy Efficiency: A New National Commitment?" CRS Issue Brief, Congressional Research Service (CRS), Washington, D.C., 1993, and on Fred J. Sissine, CRS, Washington, D.C., private communication, 6 September 1996; "New Poll Finds Pessimism On Outlook For Nuclear," *Wind Energy Weekly* (American Wind Energy Association, Washington, D.C.), 26 February 1996.

73. Solar tower from Daniel B. Wood, "It Works, But Can Anyone Afford It?" *Christian Science Monitor*, 10 June 1996; Paul Gipe, *Wind Energy Comes of Age* (New York: John Wiley & Sons, 1995).

74. Kozloff and Shobowale, op. cit. note 5.

75. Ibid.; Christopher Flavin and Nicholas Lenssen, *Power Surge: Guide to the Coming Energy Revolution* (New York: W.W. Norton, 1994).

76. Olivecrona, op. cit. note 5.

77. Kozloff and Shobowale, op. cit. note 5; Neelam Mathews, "Dynamic Market Rapidly Unfolds," *Windpower Monthly*, September 1994; Neelam Mathews, "Tax Credits Just a Catalyst," *Windpower Monthly*, July 1995; Christopher Flavin, "Wind Power Growth Accelerates," in Lester R. Brown, Christopher Flavin, and Hal Kane, *Vital Signs 1996: The Trends That Are Shaping Our Future* (New York: W.W. Norton, 1996).

78. Victoria P. Summers, "Tax Treatment of Pollution Control in the European and Central Asian Economies in Transition and Other Selected Countries," in Charles E. Walker, Mark A. Bloomfield, and Margot Thorning, eds., *Strategies for Improving Environmental Quality and Increasing Economic Growth* (Washington, D.C.: Center for Policy Research, 1995);

Ronald T. McMorran and David C.L. Nellor, "Tax Policy and the Environment: Theory and Practice," IMF Working Paper, IMF, Washington, D.C., 1994; Tomasz Żylicz, "Taxation and Environment in Poland," in OECD, *Taxation and the Environment in European Economies in Transition* (Paris, 1994).

79. Ministry of Housing, Spatial Planning, and the Environment (VROM), *Accelerated Depreciation on Environmental Investment in the Netherlands* (The Hague, 1995); Peter J. Hamelink, VROM, The Hague, paper presented at the Second European Roundtable on Cleaner Production and Cleaner Products, Rotterdam, November 1995.

80. Wilkinson, op. cit. note 2; Barber et al., op. cit. note 15; donations from *Money In Politics Alert* (Center for Responsive Politics (CRP), Washington, D.C.), 7 August 1995.

81. Rainforest Action Network, "Mitsubishi in Malaysia," San Francisco, undated, APC conference <rainfor.general>, 30 November 1995; "within a decade" from "Quest for 'Green Gold'," op. cit. note 8.

82. Robin Broad, "The Political Economy of Natural Resources: Case Studies of the Indonesian and Philippine Forest Sectors," *Journal of Developing Areas*, April 1995.

83. Daniel Stiles, "Power and Patronage in the Philippines," *Cultural Survival Quarterly*, Summer 1991.

84. Indianist Missionary Council, "Another Scandal in the Extraction of Brazilian Mahogany," Brasilia, 5 August 1996, APC conference <rainfor.general>, 7 August 1996; David Robie, "Papua New Guinea: Government Gets Drilled by Australian Oil Man," InterPress Service, 24 May 1996; Greenpeace International, op. cit. note 26; Marcus Colchester, "Asia Logs Suriname," *Multinational Monitor*, November 1995.

85. Figure of $1.6 billion from CRP, "Who's Paying for this Election?" Washington, D.C., 1996; OMB, op. cit. note 13; quote from CRP, "Back Talk, Vol. 3, No. 4," Washington, D.C., APC conference <crp.pol.news>, 26 June 1996.

86. Value of oil and gas tax breaks is a Worldwatch estimate for the 3.5-year period, based on Dawn Erlandson, Jessica Few, and Gawain Kripke, "Dirty Little Secrets," FOE, Washington, D.C., 1995; contribution figures from Elissa Silverman, CRP, Washington, D.C., private communications and printouts, 8 and 16 October 1996; history of subsidizing legislation from Wilkinson, op. cit. note 2; figure of $308,848 includes donations in 1993–94 by Amax and Cyprus Minerals, companies that then merged to become Cyprus Amax Minerals.

87. Senate preference from Ned Daly, "PAC Dollars and the Mining Reform

Conferees," Taxpayer Assets Project, Washington, D.C., APC conference <list.tap-resources>, 23 September 1994.

88. Douglas Frantz, "Dole and Ethanol Industry Count on Each Other," *New York Times*, 16 April 1996; "The Mother Jones 400," *Mother Jones*, March/April 1996; Jeffrey H. Birnbaum, "The Bucks Start Here," *Time*, 24 June 1996.

89. Mancur Olson, *The Logic of Collective Action: Public Goods and the Theory of Groups* (Cambridge, Mass.: Harvard University Press, 1971).

90. Share of work force based on OECD, *Coal Prospects*, op. cit. note 41, and on OECD, *Employment Outlook—July 1996* (Paris, 1996); Judy Dempsey, "Decision Time Looms for German Energy," *Financial Times*, 9 February 1995; Philippines from Anne Counsell, "Deregulation Hurts As It Kicks In," *Financial Times*, 18 September 1996; Thomas T. Vogel, Jr., "Venezuela to Drive Up Gasoline Prices," *Wall Street Journal*, 15 April 1996; Maurice Schiff and Alberto Valdés, "The Plundering of Agriculture in Developing Countries," World Bank, Washington, D.C., 1992.

91. Philip R. Lane and Aaron Tornell, "Power Concentration and Growth," Discussion Paper No. 1720, HIER, Harvard University, Cambridge, Mass., May 1995; Paolo Mauro, "Corruption and Growth," *Quarterly Journal of Economics*, August 1995; Nigeria from Johann Graf Lambsdorff, University of Göttingen, Göttingen, Germany, private communication and printout, 3 June 1996; Aaron Sachs, "Dying for Oil," *World Watch*, May/June 1996.

92. Brazil from Lester R. Brown, Christopher Flavin, and Sandra Postel, *Saving the Planet: How To Shape An Environmentally Sustainable Global Economy* (New York: W.W. Norton, 1991); Ed Piasecki, MPC, Washington, D.C., private communication, 4 October 1996; Smith, op. cit. note 22; Farah, op. cit. note 67; OECD, *Agricultural Policies*, op. cit. note 5; Gurvich et al., op. cit. note 1; FAO, *Fertilizer Yearbook* (Rome, 1996); BP, op. cit. note 19.

93. OECD, *Energy Policies*, op. cit. note 5; environmental side effects of imported coal from Ronald P. Steenblik and Panos Coroyannikis, "Reform of Coal Policies in Western and Central Europe: Implications for the Environment," *Energy Policy*, Vol. 23, No. 6, 1995.

94. Production drop from OECD, *Energy Policies*, op. cit. note 5; David Waddington and David Parry, "Coal Policy in Britain: Economic Reality or Political Vendetta?" in Chas Critcher, Klaus Schubert, and David Waddington, eds., *Regeneration of the Coalfield Areas: Anglo-German Perspectives* (London: Pinter, 1995); OECD, *Agricultural Policies*, op. cit. note 5.

95. Waddington and Parry, op. cit. note 94.

96. Soufi and Tuddenham, op. cit. note 33; Robert Greene, "President Signs

Farm Legislation," *Philadelphia Inquirer*, 5 April, 1996.

97. Chamberlin, op. cit. note 35.

98. Koplow, op. cit. note 7; Indonesia from Einar Hope and Balbir Singh, *Energy Price Increases in Developing Countries: Case Studies of Colombia, Ghana, Indonesia, Malaysia, Turkey, and Zimbabwe*, Policy Research Working Paper 1442 (Washington, D.C.: World Bank, 1995), and from Kerr and Citroen, op. cit. note 45.

99. Targeting techniques from Margaret E. Grosh, "Toward Quantifying the Trade-off: Administrative Costs and Incidence in Targeted Programs in Latin America," in Dominique van de Walle and Kimberly Nead, eds., *Public Spending and the Poor: Theory and Evidence* (Baltimore: Johns Hopkins University Press for the World Bank, 1995); kerosene stamps from Rhamesh Bhatia, "Energy Pricing in Developing Countries: Role of Prices in Investment Allocation and Consumer Choices," in Siddayao, op. cit. note 47; Heidarian and Wu, op. cit. note 5.

100. Koplow, op. cit. note 7.

101. USDA, op. cit. note 6; Alison Maitland, "EU Agri-environment Programmes Cost £1bn," *Financial Times*, 22 May 1996.

102. Problems with targeting of U.S. programs from Faeth, op. cit. note 32; problems in Western Europe from Maitland, op. cit. note 101.

103. Robin Broad with John Cavanagh, *Plundering Paradise: The Struggle for the Environment in the Philippines* (Berkeley: University of California Press, 1993); Susan Rose-Ackerman, "Redesigning the State to Fight Corruption: Transparency, Competition, and Privatization," Viewpoint Note No. 75, World Bank, Washington, D.C., 1996.

104. F. Leslie Seidle, "Regulating Canadian Political Finance: Established Rules in a Dynamic Political System," prepared for the Round Table on Political Reform in the Mature Democracies, Tokyo, 25–27 August 1996; figure of $6 based on $1.6 billion total spending figure from CRP, op. cit. note 85.

105. Cuff et al., op. cit. note 6.

106. Dragun, op. cit. note 15; OECD, op. cit. note 4; Larsen and Shah, op. cit. note 46.

107. Watkins and Windfuhr, op. cit. note 36; Ronald Steenblik, OECD, Paris, private communication, September 24, 1996; Jeerawat Na Thalang, "Asean Shuns Corruption, Trade Link," *The Nation* (Bangkok), 26 April 1996.

108. Hilary F. French, *Partnership for the Planet: An Environmental Agenda for the United Nations*, Worldwatch Paper 126 (Washington, D.C.: Worldwatch Institute, July 1996); Gupta et al., op. cit. note 67; Smith and Wells, op. cit. note 22.

109. Broad, op. cit. note 82; Abby Yadi, "World Bank Axes Loan," *The Independent* (Port Moresby), 2 August 1996; Neville Togarewa, "World Bank Gets Its Way on Forests," *The National* (Port Moresby), 9 October 1996; William B. Magrath, Agriculture and Forestry Systems Division, World Bank, Washington, D.C., private communication, 23 July 1996.

PUBLICATION ORDER FORM
Worldwatch Papers

No. of Copies

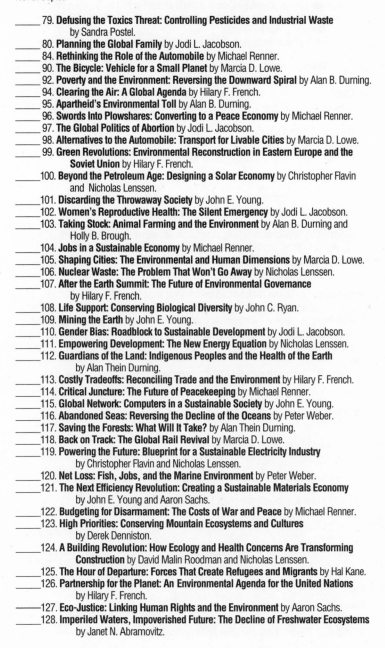

_____ 79. **Defusing the Toxics Threat: Controlling Pesticides and Industrial Waste** by Sandra Postel.
_____ 80. **Planning the Global Family** by Jodi L. Jacobson.
_____ 84. **Rethinking the Role of the Automobile** by Michael Renner.
_____ 90. **The Bicycle: Vehicle for a Small Planet** by Marcia D. Lowe.
_____ 92. **Poverty and the Environment: Reversing the Downward Spiral** by Alan B. Durning.
_____ 94. **Clearing the Air: A Global Agenda** by Hilary F. French.
_____ 95. **Apartheid's Environmental Toll** by Alan B. Durning.
_____ 96. **Swords Into Plowshares: Converting to a Peace Economy** by Michael Renner.
_____ 97. **The Global Politics of Abortion** by Jodi L. Jacobson.
_____ 98. **Alternatives to the Automobile: Transport for Livable Cities** by Marcia D. Lowe.
_____ 99. **Green Revolutions: Environmental Reconstruction in Eastern Europe and the Soviet Union** by Hilary F. French.
_____100. **Beyond the Petroleum Age: Designing a Solar Economy** by Christopher Flavin and Nicholas Lenssen.
_____101. **Discarding the Throwaway Society** by John E. Young.
_____102. **Women's Reproductive Health: The Silent Emergency** by Jodi L. Jacobson.
_____103. **Taking Stock: Animal Farming and the Environment** by Alan B. Durning and Holly B. Brough.
_____104. **Jobs in a Sustainable Economy** by Michael Renner.
_____105. **Shaping Cities: The Environmental and Human Dimensions** by Marcia D. Lowe.
_____106. **Nuclear Waste: The Problem That Won't Go Away** by Nicholas Lenssen.
_____107. **After the Earth Summit: The Future of Environmental Governance** by Hilary F. French.
_____108. **Life Support: Conserving Biological Diversity** by John C. Ryan.
_____109. **Mining the Earth** by John E. Young.
_____110. **Gender Bias: Roadblock to Sustainable Development** by Jodi L. Jacobson.
_____111. **Empowering Development: The New Energy Equation** by Nicholas Lenssen.
_____112. **Guardians of the Land: Indigenous Peoples and the Health of the Earth** by Alan Thein Durning.
_____113. **Costly Tradeoffs: Reconciling Trade and the Environment** by Hilary F. French.
_____114. **Critical Juncture: The Future of Peacekeeping** by Michael Renner.
_____115. **Global Network: Computers in a Sustainable Society** by John E. Young.
_____116. **Abandoned Seas: Reversing the Decline of the Oceans** by Peter Weber.
_____117. **Saving the Forests: What Will It Take?** by Alan Thein Durning.
_____118. **Back on Track: The Global Rail Revival** by Marcia D. Lowe.
_____119. **Powering the Future: Blueprint for a Sustainable Electricity Industry** by Christopher Flavin and Nicholas Lenssen.
_____120. **Net Loss: Fish, Jobs, and the Marine Environment** by Peter Weber.
_____121. **The Next Efficiency Revolution: Creating a Sustainable Materials Economy** by John E. Young and Aaron Sachs.
_____122. **Budgeting for Disarmament: The Costs of War and Peace** by Michael Renner.
_____123. **High Priorities: Conserving Mountain Ecosystems and Cultures** by Derek Denniston.
_____124. **A Building Revolution: How Ecology and Health Concerns Are Transforming Construction** by David Malin Roodman and Nicholas Lenssen.
_____125. **The Hour of Departure: Forces That Create Refugees and Migrants** by Hal Kane.
_____126. **Partnership for the Planet: An Environmental Agenda for the United Nations** by Hilary F. French.
——127. **Eco-Justice: Linking Human Rights and the Environment** by Aaron Sachs.
_____128. **Imperiled Waters, Impoverished Future: The Decline of Freshwater Ecosystems** by Janet N. Abramovitz.

_____ **Total Copies**

Single Copy: $5.00 • 2–5: $4.00 ea. • 6–20: $3.00 ea. • 21 or more: $2.00 ea.
Call Director of Communication, at 202-452-1999, for discounts on larger orders.

☐ *State of the World*: $13.95
The annual book used by journalists, activists, scholars, and policymakers worldwide to get a clear picture of the environmental problems we face.

☐ *Vital Signs:* $10.95
The book of trends that are shaping our future in easy to read graph and table format, with a brief commentary on each trend.

☐ Subscription to *World•Watch* magazine: $20.00 (international airmail $35.00)
Stay abreast of global environmental trends and issues with our award-winning, eminently readable bimonthly magazine.

☐ **Worldwatch Database Disk Subscription: One year for $89**
Contains global agricultural, energy, economic, environmental, social, and military indicators from all current Worldwatch publications including this Paper. Includes a mid-year update, and *Vital Signs* and *State of the World* as they are published. Can be used with Lotus 1-2-3, Quattro Pro, Excel, SuperCalc and many other spread-sheets.
Check one: _____high-density IBM-compatible or _____Macintosh

---

☐ **Send me a brochure of all Worldwatch publications.**

Make check payable to Worldwatch Institute
1776 Massachusetts Avenue, N.W., Washington, D.C. 20036-1904 USA
Please include $4 postage and handling.

Enclosed is my check or purchase order for U.S. $_____

AMEX ☐ VISA ☐ MasterCard ☐ _____
Card Number   Expiration Date

name   **daytime phone #**

address

city   **state**   **zip/country**

Phone: 202-452-1999   Fax: 202-296-7365   E-Mail: wwpub@worldwatch.org

PUBLICATION ORDER FORM
Worldwatch Papers

No. of Copies

_____ 79. **Defusing the Toxics Threat: Controlling Pesticides and Industrial Waste** by Sandra Postel.

_____ 80. **Planning the Global Family** by Jodi L. Jacobson.

_____ 84. **Rethinking the Role of the Automobile** by Michael Renner.

_____ 90. **The Bicycle: Vehicle for a Small Planet** by Marcia D. Lowe.

_____ 92. **Poverty and the Environment: Reversing the Downward Spiral** by Alan B. Durning.

_____ 94. **Clearing the Air: A Global Agenda** by Hilary F. French.

_____ 95. **Apartheid's Environmental Toll** by Alan B. Durning.

_____ 96. **Swords Into Plowshares: Converting to a Peace Economy** by Michael Renner.

_____ 97. **The Global Politics of Abortion** by Jodi L. Jacobson.

_____ 98. **Alternatives to the Automobile: Transport for Livable Cities** by Marcia D. Lowe.

_____ 99. **Green Revolutions: Environmental Reconstruction in Eastern Europe and the Soviet Union** by Hilary F. French.

_____ 100. **Beyond the Petroleum Age: Designing a Solar Economy** by Christopher Flavin and Nicholas Lenssen.

_____ 101. **Discarding the Throwaway Society** by John E. Young.

_____ 102. **Women's Reproductive Health: The Silent Emergency** by Jodi L. Jacobson.

_____ 103. **Taking Stock: Animal Farming and the Environment** by Alan B. Durning and Holly B. Brough.

_____ 104. **Jobs in a Sustainable Economy** by Michael Renner.

_____ 105. **Shaping Cities: The Environmental and Human Dimensions** by Marcia D. Lowe.

_____ 106. **Nuclear Waste: The Problem That Won't Go Away** by Nicholas Lenssen.

_____ 107. **After the Earth Summit: The Future of Environmental Governance** by Hilary F. French.

_____ 108. **Life Support: Conserving Biological Diversity** by John C. Ryan.

_____ 109. **Mining the Earth** by John E. Young.

_____ 110. **Gender Bias: Roadblock to Sustainable Development** by Jodi L. Jacobson.

_____ 111. **Empowering Development: The New Energy Equation** by Nicholas Lenssen.

_____ 112. **Guardians of the Land: Indigenous Peoples and the Health of the Earth** by Alan Thein Durning.

_____ 113. **Costly Tradeoffs: Reconciling Trade and the Environment** by Hilary F. French.

_____ 114. **Critical Juncture: The Future of Peacekeeping** by Michael Renner.

_____ 115. **Global Network: Computers in a Sustainable Society** by John E. Young.

_____ 116. **Abandoned Seas: Reversing the Decline of the Oceans** by Peter Weber.

_____ 117. **Saving the Forests: What Will It Take?** by Alan Thein Durning.

_____ 118. **Back on Track: The Global Rail Revival** by Marcia D. Lowe.

_____ 119. **Powering the Future: Blueprint for a Sustainable Electricity Industry** by Christopher Flavin and Nicholas Lenssen.

_____ 120. **Net Loss: Fish, Jobs, and the Marine Environment** by Peter Weber.

_____ 121. **The Next Efficiency Revolution: Creating a Sustainable Materials Economy** by John E. Young and Aaron Sachs.

_____ 122. **Budgeting for Disarmament: The Costs of War and Peace** by Michael Renner.

_____ 123. **High Priorities: Conserving Mountain Ecosystems and Cultures** by Derek Denniston.

_____ 124. **A Building Revolution: How Ecology and Health Concerns Are Transforming Construction** by David Malin Roodman and Nicholas Lenssen.

_____ 125. **The Hour of Departure: Forces That Create Refugees and Migrants** by Hal Kane.

_____ 126. **Partnership for the Planet: An Environmental Agenda for the United Nations** by Hilary F. French.

——— 127. **Eco-Justice: Linking Human Rights and the Environment** by Aaron Sachs.

_____ 128. **Imperiled Waters, Impoverished Future: The Decline of Freshwater Ecosystems** by Janet N. Abramovitz.

_____129. **Infecting Ourselves: How Environmental and Social Disruptions Trigger Disease** by Anne E. Platt.

_____130. **Climate of Hope: New Strategies for Stabilizing the World's Atmosphere** by Christopher Flavin and Odil Tunali.

_____131. **Shrinking Fields: Cropland Loss in a World of Eight Billion** by Gary Gardner.

_____132. **Dividing the Waters: Food Security, Ecosystem Health, and the New Politics of Scarcity** by Sandra Postel.

_____133. **Paying the Piper: Subsidies, Politics, and the Environment** by David Malin Roodman.

_____ **Total Copies**

Single Copy: $5.00 • 2–5: $4.00 ea. • 6–20: $3.00 ea. • 21 or more: $2.00 ea.
Call Director of Communication, at 202-452-1999, for discounts on larger orders.

☐ *State of the World*: **$13.95**
The annual book used by journalists, activists, scholars, and policymakers worldwide to get a clear picture of the environmental problems we face.

☐ *Vital Signs:* **$10.95**
The book of trends that are shaping our future in easy to read graph and table format, with a brief commentary on each trend.

☐ **Subscription to *World•Watch* magazine: $20.00 (international airmail $35.00)**
Stay abreast of global environmental trends and issues with our award-winning, eminently readable bimonthly magazine.

☐ **Worldwatch Database Disk Subscription: One year for $89**
Contains global agricultural, energy, economic, environmental, social, and military indicators from all current Worldwatch publications including this Paper. Includes a mid-year update, and *Vital Signs* and *State of the World* as they are published. Can be used with Lotus 1-2-3, Quattro Pro, Excel, SuperCalc and many other spread-sheets.
Check one: _____high-density IBM-compatible or _____Macintosh

---

☐ **Send me a brochure of all Worldwatch publications.**

Make check payable to Worldwatch Institute
1776 Massachusetts Avenue, N.W., Washington, D.C. 20036-1904 USA
Please include $4 postage and handling.

Enclosed is my check or purchase order for U.S. $_____

AMEX ☐ VISA ☐ MasterCard ☐ _____
                              Card Number   Expiration Date

_____
name   **daytime phone #**

_____
address

_____
city   **state   zip/country**

Phone: 202-452-1999   Fax: 202-296-7365   E-Mail: wwpub@worldwatch.org